Supervenience and Realism

DALIA DRAI
Ben-Gurion University of the Negev

Routledge
Taylor & Francis Group
LONDON AND NEW YORK

First published 1999 by Ashgate Publishing

Reissued 2018 by Routledge
2 Park Square, Milton Park, Abingdon, Oxon, OX14 4RN
711 Third Avenue, New York, NY I 0017, USA

Routledge is an imprint of the Taylor & Francis Group, an informa business

A Library of Congress record exists under LC control number: 98074200

Typeset by WordByte, P.O.B. 3102, Beer-Sheva, Israel

ISBN 13: 978-1-138-34618-5 (hbk)
ISBN 13: 978-1-138-34620-8 (pbk)
ISBN 13: 978-0-429-43742-7 (ebk)

SUPERVENIENCE AND REALISM

Contents

Introduction

The topic of this book is the relation of supervenience. This notion plays a crucial role in contemporary philosophical discussions in such diverse domains as the philosophy of mind, ethics and aesthetics. The definition of the relation of supervenience and its introduction to various weighty philosophical issues had a tremendous effect. This is most apparent in the case of the mind body problem, where a radical transformation of the very form of the question was achieved.

Traditionally the problem has often been presented (and continues to be so in many introductory texts) as follows. We are aware of two worlds. In the first there are objects which take up space, and which have mass and undergo changes which we are capable of measuring, for instance of position or temperature. This is the physical or material world, in principle observable by anyone. In the second world, by contrast, we encounter things which do not take up space and do not have volume or form. The processes of change which occur in this world are not known by everyone to the same degree. These processes—thoughts, feelings, desires—are private, not public. This is the mental world, or the world of the mind. The mind-body problem is the problem of the relation between these two worlds.

When presented as the problem of the relation between these two worlds or in more classical terms—between thinking substance and extended substance—the root of the problem can be viewed as revolving around a single question: are there two fundamentally different sorts of substance, or is extended substance identical to thinking substance?

To this central question there are two basic sorts of responses, each with several versions. According to the first, there are two fundamentally different substances, each logically independent of the other. The material world can exist without the world of mind, and the mental world of my thoughts and feelings can, at least conceptually, exist without matter. The identity of things in the mental world is not dependent on the identity of things in the physical world. Properties of physical objects, for instance color or weight, cannot, in principle, be predicated of mental objects. The two different substances belong to two different categories, and therefore any causal relation between them—if we assume one to exist—is highly problematic. This is the response known as dualism.

According to the second response there is only one kind of substance. Thinking substance is identical to extended substance. To this identity between substances there are materialist versions which recognize only physical substance, idealist versions which hold that only mental substance exists, and versions which claim that the only existing substance belongs to neither of these two categories (such as Russell's sense data). I will discuss only the materialist version of identity. According to this theory the world is the physical world. All objects are physical, all properties are physical, all events, states of affairs, and facts are physical. It follows that someone who knew all the truths of physics would know everything one could know about the world, including anything that a psychologist could know.

These two basic approaches—dualist and monist—have competed down through the centuries. Every materialist argument was countered with a dualist argument and vice versa. The situation is perhaps most appropriately described by Ramsey's principle (1990[1925]:11–12):

> In such cases it is a heuristic maxim that the truth lies not in one of the two disputed views but in some third possibility which has not yet been thought of, which we can only discover by rejecting something assumed as obvious by both the disputants.

And indeed, in criticizing what he considered the Cartesian myth, Ryle (1949) focused his attack on the assumption which he alleged was held in common by both camps, namely that the mind-body problem should be formulated in terms of categories of substances. From the fact, if such it is, that mind is not material substance, it does not follow that mind is some non-material substance, and therefore the mind-body problem is not a question of identity between substances.

From this Rylean insight an important conclusion followed. As long as the debate was conceived as one over substances, all the materialistic theses were various aspects of the same basic claim: that mental substance is identical to physical substance. And all the dualistic theses were aspects of the opposite claim: that of the non-identity between these substances. With Ryle these two attitudes shattered into many fragments—an array of these which, though related in various ways, were logically independent. The fragmentation has been fruitful, because different combinations of theses, both materialist and dualist, can now be combined in new and coherent ways. The question thus became: which fragments to combine?

In an effort to answer this question a number of important considerations have come to the fore. Many philosophers would like to preserve from dualism the notion of the autonomy of the mental. This is the claim that physics (including its expansions into chemistry and biology) will never provide an exhaustive explanation of mental phenomena. This contrasts with views, like those of Smart (1959:141–156), who argues that it is highly unlikely that only mental events can somehow escape the net of physical laws which otherwise embrace the entire universe.

Preserving the autonomy of the mental means that mental properties or states cannot be defined in, or are not reducible to, physical terms. Various logico-metaphysical arguments have been summoned in support of this anti-reductionism, for instance those purporting to show that properties such as bravery or pain cannot be identical to physical states or properties.[1] More ideological considerations have also been brought to bear, such as the putative threat to free will by a complete reduction of the mental to the physical, or perhaps a threat to the alleged superiority of humans over other animals, and over inanimate objects such as computers.

Thus it has been thought desirable to preserve from dualism the autonomy of the mental. But materialism has also offered something usually deemed worthy of preservation. As a crude first approximation we can formulate this desirable element as the claim: "The world is ultimately physical". As with the autonomy of the mental, the preservation of this thesis has also been variously motivated, both metaphysically and ideologically. The metaphysical considerations tend to run along the following line: if all the molecules (all material substance) of the world were destroyed, nothing—including minds—would be left. Even if mental objects somehow exist, they must be embodied in matter; everything existing must be in some way mediated by matter. The more ideological motivation is animated by an anti-mystical spirit: all our knowledge claims about the universe should be within the corpus of science. Claims which fail to meet this condition also fail to represent objective knowledge.

To reiterate, the challenge has been to combine fragments of both materialism and dualism which will preserve both the autonomy of the mental and the physicality of the universe. The most important step in this direction was made by Davidson.[2] Utilizing logical and semantic studies carried out completely independently of work on the mind-body problem, Davidson concluded that the role of events in our conceptual framework is considerably closer to the role of objects than at first appears. And since our ontology is supposed ultimately to reflect the logical structure of our language, he concluded that events are as much a part of our ontology as objects.

According to Davidson then, events, like objects, are property-bearing individuals. Among the various properties which events have, Davidson made a technical but important distinction. Events can be variously described. Extensional properties of events, however, can be ascribed to events independently of any description of the event. In other words, the proposition that they belong to an event is true under any description of that event. In contrast, intentional properties can be ascribed to an event only under a particular description of that event, while under some other description that ascription could be false.

This can be illustrated with an example of a simple event: Joe is running to the bus stop. Assuming that the event took place in Jerusalem, the fact of its having taken place there is not dependent on any description of it. But the question whether the event is, say, surprising, is indeed dependent on its description. Under the brief description above, the event is in no way surprising. If we add to the description, however, that it took place on Saturday when there is no bus service in Jerusalem, the property "surprising" is ascribable to it. Thus the question whether the event is surprising depends on our choice of description.

By using the ontology of events, as well as the distinction between intentional and extensional properties, Davidson suggested a combination of fragments from the old mind-body discussion which would in his view preserve both the autonomy of the mental and the physicality of the world. From the various materialist theses Davidson opted for the following: every mental event is identical to a physical event (the identity thesis). But he rejected the materialist thesis that every mental property is identical to a physical property. In this way Davidson was able to preserve the dualist thesis of the autonomy of the mental.

Davidson's success in combining the two theses coherently was due to his distinction between extensional and intentional events. Every mental event is identical to a physical event, despite the fact that the physical description of the event is entirely different from the mental description. There is no contradiction because identity is an extensional property or relation holding between events. On the other hand, physics cannot hope to explain even a single mental event, since the explanations of physics are of events under physical and not mental descriptions. Since explanation is an intentional relation between events, there is no contradiction with the thesis of identity. Davidson not only showed that the identity thesis is compatible with the autonomy of the mental, he even deduced it from assumptions about causality and lawfulness (we will not enter into this deduction).

Davidson and others consider the importance of the identity thesis as residing precisely in its having enabled the combination of the correct element of materialism (the physicality of the world) with the correct element in dualism (the autonomy of the mental). The identity thesis undoubtedly preserves the autonomy of the mental. But does it preserve the physicality of the world? On the face of it it seems so, since if all events are physical then the world is physical. In a world without matter there would be no physical events and therefore no mental events—precisely the physicalist intuition which we wished to preserve.

Here, however, I disagree with Davidson. As I will explain, his identity thesis actually captures only a small part of the physicalist intuition, and leaves out what any physicalist, including Davidson himself, would wish to claim.

On the strongest reading of the identity thesis every individual (event or object) is physical. These individuals have physical properties, and some have mental properties as well. Davidson's identity thesis leaves entirely open the possibility that mental properties will be entirely independent of physical properties. In other words, the relation between the physical properties of an object and its mental properties can be like the relation between the weight of an object and its color. There is an identity thesis for objects having color and objects having weight: any having the one must have the other. Nevertheless there is an absolute independence between color and weight; any combination between a particular color and a particular weight is possible. Such an independence is not acceptable to any physicalist, who would require a much stronger anchoring of the mental realm within the physical.

In my view, no identity thesis can ensure the desired dependence of the mental on the physical without undermining the autonomy of the mental. This is because anyone who adopts some identity thesis between the mental and the physical is faced with the following dilemma: either the identity holds between property-bearing individuals, or else it holds between the properties themselves. If the identity holds between individuals (for example, if the thesis is that all objects or events are physical) then the difficulty mentioned earlier arises: while for some individuals there are both mental and physical properties, there is no necessary connection between them. On the other hand, to claim an identity between actual properties would be to claim too much. The identity between mental and physical properties would mean a reduction of the mental to the physical, thereby negating the autonomy of the mental.

This dilemma faces any identity thesis and it can be expressed in Fregean terms. If we claim an identity between the referents of expressions we will have said too little, while if we draw the identity between senses of expressions we will have said too much. It seems, then, that in order to formulate the mind-body problem we have to give up not only the notion of substance but also the relation of identity. The illusion that Davidson's identity thesis ensures physicalism is a result of our wavering between a Davidsonian understanding of events as individuals and our pre-Davidsonian understanding of events as properties (or facts). When we say that the identity thesis preserves the autonomy of the mental we are relying on a Davidsonian understanding of events, while when we say that it preserves the physicality of the world we are momentarily relapsing to our pre-Davidsonian understanding.

It is exactly here that the notion of supervenience does the work which Davidson mistakenly supposed could be done by the notion of identity. The relation we need between the physical and the mental is a kind of determination. The physicalist cannot rest content with the claim that individuals bearing mental properties also have physical properties. Rather, he or she will want to argue that the mental properties of individuals are *determined* by physical properties. Let us recall that this determination of mental properties has to exist without any identity between mental and physical properties. This sort of determination can be elucidated by the notion of supervenience. The mental supervenes on the physical in the following sense: if two people have no physical difference between them. If, that is, they behave identically, appear identical, and have identical brain structures, then they must be in exactly the same mental state.[3]

The thesis of supervenience expresses a strong dependence between the complex of mental and the complex of physical properties, without committing itself to any dependence between a particular mental property and a physical property. This allows for the maximum physicality, as it were, without losing the autonomy of the mental. In addition, the supervenience on the accepted discourse about the physical, grants the mental discourse a sort of rubber stamp of legitimacy. Hence the great popularity of this thesis in recent years.

But at what price is this rubber stamp acquired? That is the main question of this book and it arises also in ethics. On the one hand there is a naturalist tendency to grant legitimacy to ethical discourse simply by identifying ethical and natural predicates. On this view ethical facts are nothing but natural facts. They are on a par both ontologically and epistemically: a similar ontological status is granted to the facts of ethics and to those of science; and just as the interaction between us and the natural facts explains how scientific knowledge is possible, so the interaction between us and moral facts can explain how moral knowledge is possible.

This extreme naturalist position has been on the receiving end of much criticism, most of which has been a series of variations on the theme of

Moore's open question argument. That argument was aimed at any naturalist definition of the predicate "good". Let us assume that a certain naturalist proposal has been put forward to define the predicate "good" as *N*, *N* being a natural predicate. The proposition "Any action which is *N* is *N*" is of course trivial, but the proposition that an action which is *N* is also good is informative. It is always possible to ask about a particular action which we know to be *N* if it is good. Such a question would not betray linguistic incompetence as would the question "Is every action which is *N*, *N* ?" The first is an open question. The fact that the substitution of "good" for *N* transforms a trivial question into an open one shows in Moore's view that *N* cannot be the definition of "good".

Two kinds of response have been directed against Moore's argument. According to the first, "All *N* are good" is a complicated analytic proposition, and therefore the question whether an action which is *N* is good is an open question in the same sense in which the question whether Goldbach's Conjecture is true is an open question. According to the second response, the question is open because the proposition that all *N* are good is not analytic and not even a matter for a priori inquiry. Nevertheless, it is a necessary proposition just as "Water = H_2O" is a necessary proposition which is neither analytic nor a matter of a priori knowledge.

I will not enter here into a discussion of the adequacy of the respective responses. What is important to notice is that if we advocate the thesis of supervenience of moral predicates on natural ones, the entire question never arises. The strong relation between the moral and the natural is retained without any proposition of the sort "All *N* are good" being true, so that the problem of the status of such propositions simply disappears.

And just as in philosophy of mind, here too supervenience enables the preservation of the ethical in a natural world without falling vulnerable to anti-reductionist arguments. Therefore here too there is a question of what we are committed to when we adopt a position affirming determination but denying reduction. As I already said, that is the question to which this book is dedicated. In brief, the answer which I will develop is that in both cases this position commits us to an anti-realist approach with regard to the supervenient domains.

The first chapter of this book distinguishes between different concepts of supervenience and shows that all of them express determination of one domain by the other. The second chapter attempts to demonstrate that the notion of supervenience without reduction is coherent. As such it is a viable, indeed attractive, candidate for the articulation of the relation between the mental and the physical and between the moral and natural domains. In the third chapter I make this assumption of non-reductive supervenience for ethics and then investigate how it can be explained. The conclusion of the chapter is that the best explanation for this assumption commits us to an anti-realist view of the moral domain. The fourth chapter argues similarly with regard to the mental. The fifth chapter compares the anti-realist positions in ethics and in the philosophy of mind, and tentatively explores other areas where the moves of the previous chapters can be applied.

Notes

1 See for instance Fodor (1974) and Putnam (1975).
2 For instance in "Mental Events", Davidson (1982).
3 In the next chapter I deal with various versions of supervenience which reflect different modal readings of this characterization of the relation.

1 Supervenience

1.1 Definitions of Supervenience

Supervenience is a relation between two sets of predicates. The set of predicates *A* supervenes on the set of predicates *B* if and only if there is no difference with respect to the predicates in *A* without there being a difference with respect to the predicates in *B*. This definition should be sharpened, and there are a number of ways of doing so. I shall distinguish between two types of supervenience: local and global. Local supervenience guarantees that there is no *A*-difference between two objects without there also being a *B*-difference between those objects. In other words, according to local supervenience the *A*-properties of an object are determined by the *B*-properties of that object. In contrast, global supervenience guarantees nothing as to the relations between the *A*-properties and the *B*-properties of a specific object. In fact, as I will show later, it does not even guarantee that *A*-properties and *B*-properties apply to the same objects. According to global supervenience, the set of *B*-truths[1] determines the set of *A*-truths. This implies that there are no two possible worlds which differ in their *A*-truths but not in their *B*-truths. I shall define four types of local supervenience in this section, and will treat global supervenience in the next.

Let *W* be a set of possible worlds, and $A=\{A_1, A_2...\}$ and $B=\{B_1, B_2...\}$, two sets of predicates. I shall now define four types of supervenience of *A* on *B* and supply some examples.

Supervenience$_1$: two objects that are indiscernible with respect to *B*-predicates are also indiscernible with respect to *A*-predicates. In other words, if a certain object has the property A_i and another object does not have that property, then there is a property in *B* which applies to the first object but not to the second.

A_i and B_i are properties that apply to an object at a certain point in time; they may stop applying to it. Hence, there are two ways of understanding supervenience$_1$. According to the first interpretation, for any time t, if two objects differ in any *A*-property at time t, then they also differ in a *B*-property at time t. According to the second interpretation, if an object x has the property A_i at time t_1 and an object y does not have that property at time t_2, then there is a property B_i in *B* such that x has B_i at t_1 and y does not have B_i at t_2. Since the second interpretation is more general, I shall understand supervenience$_1$ according to it.

Supervenience$_2$ in every possible world, two objects that are indiscernible with respect to *B*-predicates are also indiscernible with respect to *A*-predicates. Supervenience$_2$ holds when supervenience$_1$ holds in every possible world. Kim (1984) calls this weak supervenience. In the same paper he proposes another definition of supervenience$_2$:

> *A* weakly supervenes on *B* if and only if necessarily for any property *F* in *A*, if an object *x* has *F*, then there exists a property *G* in *B* such that *x* has *G*, and if any *y* has *G* it has *F*. (1984:164)[2]

Kim claims that the two definitions are equivalent. I will show that the second entails the first, but that the reverse only holds when an unwarranted assumption about the nature of set *B* is made.

Suppose that the second definition is true of a certain domain. Let *x* and *y* be two objects that are *B*-indiscernible; I will show that they are also *A*-indiscernible. For every property A_i in *A* that *x* has, there is, according to the second definition, a property B_i in *B* such that *x* is B_i, and everything that is B_i is also A_i. Since *x* and *y* are *B*-indiscernible, *y* is also B_i, and since all the B_is are A_is, *y* is A_i. Thus, I have shown that every property in *A* that applies to *x* also applies to *y*; *x* and *y* are also *A*-indiscernible.

Suppose now that the first definition holds. Can we then conclude that the second definition holds as well? Only if we assume that any Boolean combination of *B*-predicates (even an infinite one) also belongs to set *B*. On this assumption, for every *x* and A_i the conjunction of all the *B*-predicates that apply to *x* is the predicate B_i required by the definition. In section 1.3 I will show that this assumption is wrong, and argue that there is no reason why the discussion of the supervenience of *A* on *B* should be limited to cases in which *B* is closed under all the Boolean combinations. Once this assumption is rejected, however, it is no longer true that the two definitions are equivalent. Henceforth, whenever I mention supervenience$_2$ I shall refer to the first definition.

Supervenience$_3$: two possible objects that are indiscernible with respect to *B* are also indiscernible with respect to *A*. Kim (1984:165) calls this concept strong supervenience. He provides another definition for this notion of supervenience too; the two definitions fail to be equivalent for the same reason as that mentioned above in the case of supervenience$_2$.

Supervenience$_4$: no change with respect to *B* can occur without a change with respect to *A* occurring as well. In other words, no object can change with respect to *B*-predicates without also changing with respect to *A*-predicates.

Supervenience$_1$ involves no modal operators; supervenience$_2$ involves a modal operator that ranges over sentences only; and supervenience$_3$ involves quantifying over possible objects as well as over possible worlds. This makes it possible to attribute to an object modal properties that apply to it independently of how it is described, and thus to let the modal operator range over open formulae as well. This difference between supervenience$_2$ and supervenience$_3$ is significant, since philosophers who accept modality in the propositional calculus but reject it in the predicate calculus (e.g., Quine, 1953) will treat supervenience$_2$ but not supervenience$_3$ as meaningful.

The disadvantage of supervenience$_2$, however, is that it does not afford the drawing of comparisons between objects across possible worlds. Yet we want to draw such comparisons in many domains in which supervenience claims are made. Take for example the supervenience of aesthetic predicates on non-aesthetic ones. Here we want to assert more than just supervenience$_2$. We say that two paintings that are identical in their physical properties are necessarily equally beautiful. But we also want to make such counterfactual statements as that if certain changes occurred in the world that did not affect the physical properties of a picture, then that picture would remain as beautiful as it was before those changes occurred; or that if additional lines were drawn in a picture so that it looked like a work by Picasso, then that picture would be as beautiful as a work by Picasso. In both cases we compare the picture as it is in our world with the picture as it is in another possible world. Supervenience$_3$, which quantifies over possible objects, allows us to draw such comparisons.

Supervenience$_4$ can be strengthened by the addition of modal operators, thus allowing the claim that not only is there no object in our world that can undergo a change with respect to *A* without changing with respect to *B*, but there is no such object in any other possible world either. I will ignore this strong version of supervenience$_4$ for two reasons: first, because it seems to me that supervenience$_4$ expresses an intuition of determinacy even without the addition of modality. And second, because the modal interpretation of supervenience$_4$ can be read into its definition even without positing the quantification over possible worlds. The definition refers to the possibility of objects undergoing certain changes. Now in my opinion, the best way to interpret the claim that an object *x* can change with respect to a property *P* is to understand it as the claim that such changes do in fact take place—i.e., that objects like *x* do sometimes change with respect to *P*. This definition is somewhat vague since it appeals to the notion of similarity. Two objects (or changes) can be similar in the context of physical theory but different in the context of biological or psychological theory (Putnam, 1975:239). When the context determines the relevant notion of similarity, the modal operator adds nothing to the content of supervenience$_4$.

Let me now turn to examining the logical relations between the four concepts I have defined. Obviously, supervenience$_3$ entails supervenience$_2$, and supervenience$_2$ entails supervenience$_1$. I will now show that these relations of entailment are not reversible, and that these are therefore three distinct notions of supervenience. There may be sets of predicates for which supervenience$_1$ holds but not supervenience$_2$. For example:

B={*x*'s identity number is 1, etc.}

A={*x*'s birthday is 1900, etc.}.

Since no two people have the same identity number, *A* supervenes$_1$ on *B*. But in a possible world where siblings have the same identity number, two brothers who were not born in the same year are indiscernible with respect to *B*-predicates, yet discernible with respect to *A*-predicates. Hence *A* does not supervene$_2$ on *B*. This example shows that there is no entailment from supervenience$_1$ to supervenience$_2$.

There may be two sets of predicates for which supervenience$_2$ holds but supervenience$_3$ does not. Here is one example: *B* includes predicates that ascribe a time and place of birth to people, and *A*={*x* is a male, *x* is a female}. Since there is no possible world in which two people were born at the same time and place, *A* supervenes$_2$ on *B*. Let us examine a possible world *w* in which a male child was born at the same time and place as me. The child in *w* and I in this world are two possible objects that are indiscernible with respect to *B*-predicates (born at the same time and place), yet are discernible with respect to *A*-predicates (one is a male, the other a female). Hence supervenience$_3$ does not hold, and supervenience$_2$ is seen not to entail supervenience$_3$.

We have seen that supervenience$_3$ is stronger than supervenience$_2$, and supervenience$_2$ is stronger than supervenience$_1$. It is harder to characterize the relations between supervenience$_4$ and the other theses. The following example, however, shows that supervenience$_4$ does not entail the other kinds of supervenience. The temperature of a rod cannot change without its length changing accordingly. Hence, the temperature of a rod supervenes$_4$ on its length. Yet it is clear that temperature does not supervene$_1$ on length, since there are rods in the world that are identical in length but not in temperature. Hence, supervenience$_2$ and supervenience$_3$ do not hold either.

I will now show that supervenience$_4$ is entailed by supervenience$_1$: if supervenience$_4$ does not hold, then there is an object *x* which has undergone an *A*-change without undergoing a *B*-change. Hence *x* at time *t* and *x* at time *t** (some time after the occurrence of the change) are indiscernible with respect to *B*-predicates, but discernible with respect to *A*-predicates—which contradicts supervenience$_1$.

The deduction of supervenience$_4$ from supervenience$_1$ is made possible by the fact that supervenience$_1$ is a generalization that applies to any ordered pair of objects, whereas supervenience$_4$ is a special case of that generalization and applies only to the ordered pairs in which the first item is identical to the second. Limiting supervenience$_1$ to pairs of objects in which the first item is not identical to the second would yield the following statement: two different objects which are indiscernible with respect to B are also indiscernible with respect to A. This statement which I shall call supervenience$_1$*, poses constraints on the differences between objects. In contrast, supervenience$_4$ (which is supervenience$_1$ limited to pairs of identical objects) expresses constraints on the changes which objects can undergo. According to supervenience$_1$*, there is no A-difference without a B-difference, and according to supervenience$_4$, there is no A-change without a B-change. On the face of it, these two theses are unrelated; in fact, however, there is an important conceptual link between them. First, supervenience$_2$*—the claim that supervenience$_1$* is necessary—entails supervenience$_4$. Second, supervenience$_4$ can be proved form supervenience$_1$* with the help of a thought experiment. Here are the proofs of both entailments.

Suppose that supervenience$_2$* is true. In order to prove the truth of supervenience$_4$, I shall assume its negation. If supervenience$_4$ is false, then there is an object x that underwent an A-change without undergoing a B-change. In other words, there is an A-predicate that applies to x at t_1 but not at t_2, even though the same B-predicates apply to x at both times. Suppose now that it is possible for x to have a B-doppelganger, that is, an object that is not numerically identical to x but is indiscernible from it with respect to B-predicates.[3] Consider a world w in which y is x's B-doppelganger. Since supervenience$_2$* holds, x at t_1 and y are indiscernible with respect to A-predicates as well. But x at t_2 is also y's doppelganger; hence x at t_2 and y are indiscernible with respect to A-predicates. It follows that x at t_1 and x at t_2 are indiscernible with respect to A-predicates—and this contradicts the assumption that x has undergone a change in A-predicates between t_1 and t_2.

I have shown that supervenience$_4$ follows from supervenience$_2$*. I will now demonstrate that it is possible, with the help of a thought experiment, to use a similar proof to deduce supervenience$_4$ from the weaker supervenience$_1$*. Again, let us start with an x that has undergone an A-change without undergoing a B-change. Suppose that y is a B-doppelganger of x that exists in our world, albeit on a distant star. Using the same line of argument as above, we may prove that x has not undergone an A-change, and hence that supervenience$_4$ is true. Note that in establishing the truth of supervenience$_4$ on the basis of supervenience$_2$*, I have assumed that x's possible doppelganger exists in the actual world. I will now assume that the truth of supervenience$_4$ does not hang on the existence of such a doppelganger. This assumption makes sense: for why should the possibility of an object undergoing change hang on the existence of a doppelganger on some distant star? The assumption saves us the need to justify the claim that such a doppelganger actually exists in our world, thereby allowing the deduction of supervenience$_4$ from supervenience$_1$*. Thus, I have shown that the deduction of supervenience$_4$ from supervenience$_1$ is not only formal: constraints on the differences between objects yield constraints on the changes which an object may undergo.

In sum, here are the logical relations between the four theses of supervenience: supervenience$_3$ → supervenience$_2$ → supervenience$_1$ → supervenience$_4$. In what follows, I shall examine which theses capture our intuition of determinacy.

1.2 Global Supervenience

In order to see why we need a global notion of supervenience, consider the following problem. For the sake of the argument, let us assume with Burge (1979) and Putnam (1975) that the content of speakers' thoughts depends, among other things, on their environment. According to Burge, the content of a thought depends on the linguistic community to which the speaker belongs, and according to Putnam, on the molecular make up of things in the speaker's environment. In both cases, the content of a thought does not depend solely on the physical state of the speaker. Since the content of a speaker's thoughts is part of his or her mental state, it follows that the speaker's mental state is not a function of his or her physical state only.[4] Does this externalist conclusion contradict the thesis of the supervenience of the mental on the physical?

Not necessarily. All that follows from it is that the mental states of speakers do not supervene on the speakers' physical properties only, but also on their physical relations to things in their surroundings. As long as these relations are of a physical nature, this involves no contradiction with the thesis of supervenience. A similar line of argument appears in discussions about the supervenience of aesthetic properties on non-aesthetic ones. It may seem at first that the thesis of the supervenience of aesthetic properties on non-aesthetic properties can be refuted thus: two pictures may be identical in their intrinsic physical properties yet differ in their aesthetic value—for example, if one is authentic whereas the other is a fake, or if they are associated with different schools of art, or if they are displayed in different locations. Here too it may rightly be claimed that there is no contradiction with the supervenience thesis as long as the aesthetic differences between the pictures depend on the non-aesthetic relations between the pictures on one hand, and other objects in the world on the other.

But while this argument does show that supervenience and externalism are compatible, by allowing relations to be included within the set of base predicates, it raises another difficulty: for when a set of predicates is defined so as to allow for the description of an object under so many aspects, it makes sense to assume that it will afford a unique description of that object. For instance, adding to a picture's intrinsic features properties about its producer and the time and place at which it was created ensures that there will be no other picture with the same properties. In this case, both supervenience$_1$ and supervenience$_2$ are true—but trivial. The problem, then, is that we have only salvaged the supervenience thesis at the price of trivializing it. I shall discuss cases of trivial supervenience in depth later;[5] but first, let me show how a global notion of supervenience solves this problem.

The global definition of supervenience does not refer to objects but to possible worlds. Here is Haugeland's (1982:97) definition of global supervenience: *A* globally supervenes on *B* if, for any two possible worlds, the following holds: if there is a sentence in language *A* that is true in the first world but false in the second, then there is a sentence in language *B* that is true in the first world but false in the second. (By "language *A*" I mean the language constituted by the set of *A*-predicates.)

This definition reflects an intuition of determinacy, whereby the world could not be different with respect to *A* without being different with respect to *B*. This notion of supervenience solves the problem of trivial supervenience, since it does not follow from the fact that local supervenience is trivial that global supervenience is trivial as well. Even if the set of *B*-predicates is such that there are no two different objects, in any possible world, that are indiscernible with respect to *B*, there may still be two possible worlds that are indiscernible with respect to language *B*. The question whether these worlds are indiscernible with respect to language *A* as well is by no means trivial. If the answer to this question is positive, then *A* globally supervenes on *B*.

According to Haugeland, the main advantage of the global notion of supervenience is that, in contrast with the local notion, it does not imply any identity thesis. In its most general sense, an identity thesis rejects dualism, namely, the claim that there are two different categories of objects, one, of objects which only satisfy *A*-predicates, and the other, of objects which only satisfy *B*-predicates. Armed with this general definition, let us examine the relations of entailment between the identity thesis and local supervenience.

Let there be two sets of predicates, the first consisting of $A_1, A_2, \ldots A_n, \ldots$ and the second, of $B_1, B_2, \ldots B_n, \ldots$. According to the identity thesis, it is not the case that there are two separate realms of objects, those which bear the properties of the first set and those which bear the properties of the second. Any object can in principle bear properties from both sets. This claim is consistent with the predicates of the two sets being mutually independent—as is the case, for example, if the predicates of the first set assign color to objects and the predicates of the second, geometric shape to those same objects. It is also consistent with the two categories of predicates being mutually dependent, as is the case, for example, if the predicates of the first set assign color to objects and the predicates of the second refer to wavelengths. Hence, the supervenience thesis does not follow from the identity thesis.[6]

Does the identity thesis follow from the thesis of local supervenience? Haugeland (1982:96) answers that it does; I believe that the answer is more complex. To see why, suppose that the identity thesis is not true, and that there are two sets of objects: those to which only *A*-properties apply, and those to which only *B*-properties apply. In such a case, it will not always be true that local supervenience does not hold: any two objects that are indiscernible with respect to *B* are also indiscernible with respect to *A*, since no *A*-property distinguishes between them. On the other hand, two objects that are discernible with respect to *A* are indiscernible with respect to *B*. In a case such as the one we are envisaging, then, local supervenience fails to hold if and only if there are two objects that are discernible with respect to *A*.[7] If all the objects to which the *A*-properties apply are indiscernible with respect to these properties, the thesis of local supervenience holds in spite of the fact that the identity thesis does not. Apart from this marginal case (I will go over the grounds for disregarding it in section 1.4), Haugeland's claim that local supervenience entails the identity thesis is correct.

In contrast, global supervenience can hold in cases in which the identity thesis is false. An example by Haugeland illustrates this: the set of possible worlds W is a set of white paper sheets on each of which is drawn a finite number of loops. On each sheet, there is a polar system of coordinates. The *A*-predicates describe properties of the loops and relations between them, such as *x* is a circle, *x* is a square, *x* encircles *y*, *x* encircles a wider area than *y*, etc. The *B*-predicates describe the properties of arrows and the relations between them and real numbers: *z* is the sum of *x* and *y*; *z* is the product of *x* and *y*; and *x* is the arrow that starts at the origin of the coordinates, has an angle of *y* degrees from the northern axis, and is colored black at a point that lies *z* units away from the origin. The *A*-predicates globally supervene on the *B*-predicates, since two sheets that can be discerned in terms of the language of loops can also be discerned in terms of the language of arrows. For example, if there is a circle on the first sheet but none on the second, then necessarily there is a black point on the first sheet but none on the second (or vice versa). Having found such a point, we may draw an arrow up to it from the origin of the coordinates. Suppose that arrow to have an angle of *y* degrees from the northern axis and to be *z* units long. The sentence "there is an arrow *x* that has an angle of *y* degrees and is black at a point that is at a distance *z* from the origin of the coordinates" is true relative to the first sheet but false relative to the second. Hence, the identity thesis is clearly false in this case despite the fact that global supervenience holds: the objects to which *A*-predicates apply are loops, and those to which *B*-predicates apply are arrows.

Whether we choose to say that the application of *B*-predicates to loops is meaningless or that it is always false, it is clear that local supervenience (however defined) does not hold. For any two loops that are discernible in terms of language *A* (for example, one is a square and the other a circle), there is no *B*-predicate that applies to the one but not to the other, for the simple reason that no *B*-predicate applies to loops at all.

Haugeland claims that the importance of the global notion of supervenience is revealed in the context of the issue of the relations between the mental and the physical. According to him, mental events cannot be identified with physical events. The concept of global supervenience enables us to safeguard the intuition that the domain of mental events is determined by the domain of physical events, without having to commit ourselves to an identity thesis à la Davidson. Even if Haugeland's arguments against the identity of the mental and the physical are inconclusive, he is right about the fact that our intuition of determinacy is global, and does not imply the identity thesis. For,

> The individuals or "tokens" of which our sentences are true are just as "relative" to the levels of description as are the kinds or "types" into which those sentences sort them...the individuals we can discuss in one way of talking need not be identified with the individuals we can discuss in another way of talking, even if the latter way of talking is somehow basic and comprehensive. (Haugeland, 1982:101)

Another advantage of the global notion of supervenience is that it enables us to formulate a thesis of the supervenience of one set of propositions on another set of propositions. This, in turn, enables us to view the supervenience of the set of *A*-predicates on the set of *B*-predicates as a special case of the supervenience of language *A* on language *B*. The two following examples elucidate this point.

In the first example, language *A* but not language *B* includes the modal (sentential) operators "possibly *p*" and "necessarily *p*". This is the only difference between the two languages. Since the difference between the languages does not lie in their being constituted of different sets of predicates, any supervenience thesis that is formulated in terms of the relations between sets of predicates is empty here. However, the question whether the world could have been different with respect to some modal proposition without differing in respect to any non-modal proposition is not at all empty. This question can be formulated in terms of the definition of global supervenience: is language *A* globally supervenient on language *B?* In other words, are there two possible worlds such that exactly the same non-modal sentences hold in both, but there is a modal sentence that holds in one and not in the other?

In the second example, language *A* includes everything that is included in language *B*, and in addition it includes sentences that describe natural laws. Here again, the difference between the two languages does not lie in their constituent predicates, but in the way propositions are built in each language. The thesis that laws of nature do not describe additional facts about the world can be formulated in terms of the concept of global supervenience: if all the propositions that are not laws of nature have the same truth-value in two possible worlds, then so do all the laws of nature in those two worlds.

I shall end this section by examining the logical relations between local and global supervenience. Haugeland's example shows that global supervenience does not entail any type of local supervenience. I will now show that supervenience$_2$ does not entail global supervenience, and that, a fortiori, nor do the weaker supervenience$_1$ and supervenience$_4$. Following Lewis (1986:15), imagine a moral theory according to which an act is good iff it corresponds to God's will. In any possible world, God's will is only sensitive to the natural features of an act. However, God wills different acts in different worlds.

According to this view (which is, of course, coherent), the moral properties of an act supervene$_2$ on its natural properties. However, global supervenience does not hold here: for there may be two possible worlds, w_1 and w_2, which are indiscernible with respect to their natural properties yet differ with respect to their description in the language of the moral theory. This difference results from the fact that God may want people in w_1 to praise Him, but people in w_2 to curse Him. Hence, supervenience$_2$ does not entail global supervenience.

In this example, supervenience$_3$ does not hold. Hence, it still remains to be seen whether or not supervenience$_3$—which is the strongest notion of supervenience—entails global supervenience. As I show below, as long as no assumptions are made about the nature of the set of predicates and the set of possible worlds, supervenience$_3$—like the other theses of local supervenience—does not entail global supervenience. Here is a simple example in which supervenience$_3$ holds but global supervenience does not.

Let the set of possible worlds be the set of subsets of the natural numbers. Set *A* includes only one predicate: "*x* is an even number". Set *B* includes the following predicates: $x=2, x=4, x=6, x=8\ldots$ Set *A* locally supervenes (under all the versions of local supervenience) on set *B*, but global supervenience does not hold. To see this, examine the following two possible worlds:

$w_1 = \{\text{the set of all even numbers}\}$

$w_2 = W_1 \cup \{3\}$

w_1 and w_2 are indiscernible with respect to language *B:* every sentence that is true in W_1 is also true in w_2 and vice versa. However, they are discernible with respect to language *A*, since the sentence "all objects are even" is true in the former but false in the latter. Conclusion: as long as no constraints are posed on the set of possible worlds and on the set of predicates, supervenience$_3$ does not entail global supervenience.

The entailment does hold, however, if we add two general premises:

Premise I (the compactness premise): the set of possible worlds can be represented by the class of models which satisfies the compactness theorem. Specifically, for an infinite set of sentences *G*, if for every finite subset of *G* there is a model in the class which satisfies that subset, then there is a model in the class which satisfies *G*.

Two points should be stressed. First, it makes sense to require that a class which represents possibilities should satisfy the compactness premise. Offhand, at least, it is difficult to come up with an example of a world such that there is no upper bound to the set of properties that it can satisfy simultaneously, yet at the same time it cannot satisfy an infinite set of those properties. Second, compactness is weaker than elementariness. *A* class of models is elementary if it can be characterized by a first-order theory, i.e., if there is a theory *T* such that a model belongs to the class iff it satisfies *T*. As I show in the appendix to this chapter (section 1.5), the set of models that represent physical possibility is not an elementary class, but this does not preclude it from satisfying the compactness theorem. Hence, not every class of models that satisfies the compactness theorem is elementary.

Consider, for example, the class of all the models of Peano's axioms: it is elementary. Subtract from it all the models that are not denumerable: the resulting class is no longer elementary, yet still satisfies the compactness theorem. The reason for this is that for every non-denumerable model that satisfies *G*, there is an denumerable model that also satisfies *G* (according to Skolem-Lowenheim's theorem).[8]

Premise II (the premise of externalism): the sets of predicates are closed under the following operator: if $P_1 \ldots P_n$ are predicates of *A* (or *B*), then any formula with one free variable formed with $P_1 \ldots P_n$ also belongs to *A* (or *B*). This means that the sets of predicates *A* and *B* are better defined as closures (in a first-order language) of the more basic sets of predicates.

It is important to note that my claim is not that this premise is necessary to discussions about supervenience; on the contrary, I show in the next section that no such premise is necessary. I only claim that it is reasonable to work with this premise in the two fields which I shall be discussing, namely, the mental and the moral. In both, if we do not include predicates that have to do with the object's environment in the set of base predicates, then the claim of supervenience is blatantly false. The only way to express the intuition that one set of predicates determines the other is to add the premise of externalism.

With these two premises, I may now proceed to show that global supervenience can be deduced from supervenience$_3$. Suppose that supervenience$_3$ holds, and that w_1 and w_2 are two possible worlds in which a theory *B* is true. In other words, every sentence in language *B* that is true in w_1 is also true in w_2. Suppose further that a is an object in w_1, and that $P_1 \ldots P_n \ldots$ is the set of all the formulae that are true of a in w_1. Examine the following series of theories (*c* is an individual constant that is not part of languages *A* and *B*):

$$P_1c \text{ U } \{\text{all the sentences in language } A \text{ that are true in } w_2\}.$$

|

|

$$P_1c\&P_2c\ldots\&P_nc \text{ U } \{\text{all the sentences in language } A \text{ that are true in } w_2\}.$$

|

Every term in the series is a consistent set of sentences, since w_2 satisfies it; and the same goes for every finite number of terms in the series, since each term includes the preceding one. Hence, every set is consistent. This means that there is a model of all the sentences in language *A* that are true in w_2, which includes an object *b* that has all the *B*-properties that *a* has in w_1. The compactness premise guarantees that this model represents a possible world w_3 which belongs to set *w*. Hence, with the help of supervenience$_3$ we can infer that a and b have the same *A*-properties.

Let *p* be a proposition in language *A* that is true in w_1. The proposition $x=x\&p$ is true of *a* in w_1. Since all the formulae that are true of *a* in w_1 are also true of *b* in w_3, $x=x\&p$ is true of *b* in w_3. Hence, *p* is true in w_3 (assuming the premise of externalism). It follows that w_1 and w_3 have the same *A* theory; and since w_3 was stipulated to have the same *A* theory as w_2, it follows in turn that w_2 has the same *A* theory as w_1—which is what we set out to demonstrate.

In sum, these are the entailments that hold between the local theses of supervenience and global supervenience: global supervenience follows from supervenience$_3$ (assuming the two premises discussed above), and is logically independent from all the other theses of local supervenience.

1.3 The Nature of the Set of Base Properties

My discussion of the logical relations between the various supervenience theses was based on the assumption that the set of *B*-predicates is not subject to any closure constraint. In other words, no operation on predicates or properties satisfies the following condition: applying it to *B*-predicates yields a predicate or property that necessarily belongs to *B*. This is a crucial assumption, for different supervenience theses merge according to which closure constraint is posited. Thus, for example, Kim (1979:41) claims that set *B* should be closed under infinite Boolean combinations, and concludes hence that the concept of supervenience$_2$ is equivalent to the following relation between sets of predicates *A* and *B*: necessarily for every *a* in *A* and for every *x*, if *x* is *a*, then there is a *b* in *B* such that *x* is *b*, and all the *b*s are *a*s. Kim also concludes that supervenience$_3$ is equivalent to the following concept: for every *a* in *A* and for every *x*, if *x* is *a*, then there is a *b* in *B* such that *x* is *b* and necessarily all the *b*'s are *a*'s.

My view is that in the context of discussions that are restricted to the concept of supervenience and do not deal with its relations with other concepts, closure conditions should not be automatically posited; rather, they should only be posited as a result of the discussion of specific cases, and should be restricted to the relevant domains. I shall discuss the principles that guide the choice of such conditions later, but first let me explain why it is wrong to posit in advance constraints on the sets of predicates.

Our initial question was whether a set of predicates *A* supervenes on a set *B*, and, in general, what relations prevail between these two sets. If we close the sets under certain operations, this question becomes the question of whether set *A* enriched with additional predicates supervenes on set *B* enriched with additional predicates. That, of course, is a different question from the original one.

My answer may seem simplistic, as I have not dealt with debates about supervenience in the context of specific domains. In such debates, the base set is not defined by the predicates that belong to it, but rather by a meta-predicate which all the predicates of the set satisfy. Thus, the base set in discussions of supervenience in ethics, for example, is the set of natural predicates; in the context of the mind-body problem, it is the set of physical predicates; and in discussions about Leibniz' thesis that relations are determined by the objects' properties, it is the set of all the predicates that refer to an internal property (internalism). In all these cases, the sets are not defined by a list of the predicates that belong to them, and this leaves room for less general questions, such as: does the infinite disjunction of physical predicates yield a physical predicate? Is the negation of an internal property itself an internal property? Van Cleve suggests the following principle for these cases:

> If the thesis under discussion is that *A*-properties supervene on *B*-properties, then let the base set be closed under a given operation if and only if *B*-hood is preserved by that operation. (Van Cleve, 1990:228)

This principle seems reasonable, and I shall later discuss contexts where it is indeed of use. At this stage, however, it is quite redundant. Its sole justification lies in the fact that its violation causes a shift in the topic of discussion. But this also justifies the simpler and more general principle that I presented at the beginning of this discussion—namely, that there is no need for any constraint on the nature of the sets. If the set we are interested in is that of physical properties, then it is clear that if physicality is a property that remains constant under disjunction, then the set of physical predicates will have to be closed under disjunction. If, on the other hand, we are interested in the set of simple predicates, or in those that include one disjunction only, then of course we will not allow sets which are closed under disjunction.

It is important to note that, in contrast with other kinds of operations, the requirement that the sets be closed under Boolean operations is quite harmless.[9] For the following property is true of all the concepts of supervenience that I have defined: *A* supervenes on *B* if and only if the Boolean closure of *A* supervenes on the Boolean closure of *B*. I shall prove this for supervenience$_1$; a similar proof applies to the other three concepts of supervenience.

First direction: let *A* supervene$_1$ on *B*. I shall prove that the closure of *A* (*A**) supervenes$_1$ on the closure of *B* (*B**). Suppose that *x* and *y* are indiscernible with respect to *B**. Since *B* is included in *B**, they are also indiscernible with respect to *B*. From our premise it follows that *x* and *y* are indiscernible with respect to *A*. Can they be discernible with respect to *A**? Suppose, by negation, that the answer is positive. If *x* and *y* are discernible with respect to *A**, the distinction must lie in a property that is finite (i.e., of finite length): for an infinite disjunction (or conjunction) can be true of *x* but not of *y* if and only if one of the disjuncts (or conjuncts) is true of *x* but not of *y*. Let us, then, take the simplest property—that which has the smallest possible number of connectives—with respect to which *x* and *y* are discernible, and call it ***a***. If ***a*** is a disjunction, then since *x* and *y* satisfy exactly the same disjuncts, they also satisfy the same disjunction. The same goes for conjunctions. What about negations? If ***a*** = ~***a'***, and ***a*** is true of *x* but not of *y*, then ***a'*** is true of *y* but not of *x*—which contradicts our stipulation that ***a*** is the smallest property distinguishing *x* from *y*.

Second direction: let A^* supervene$_1$ on B^*. Here is the proof that A supervenes$_1$ on B. Let x and y be two objects that are indiscernible with respect to B. Then, for the reasons mentioned above, they are also indiscernible with respect to B^*. From our premises it follows that they are indiscernible with respect to A^* (and, since A includes A^*, they are indiscernible with respect to A.[10]

This feature of Boolean operations is not true, as I shall now show, of every mechanism that combines given properties into other properties. For reasons that I shall discuss later, Bacon (1986) defines the following way of creating new properties:

> Where P_w is the extension of P at world W, and $B_w = \{P_w : P \in B\}$, B is also to contain any property Q such that $Q_w \in B_w$ for each world W. (Bacon, 1986:165)

In contrast to Boolean combinations, this diagonalization mechanism does not have the following feature: A supervenes on B if and only if the closure of A under diagonalization supervenes on the closure of B under diagonalization. This is illustrated by the following example:

The extension of B_1 in possible world w_1 is $\{x, y\ldots\}$
The extension of B_1 in possible world w_2 is $\{y\ldots\}$
The extension of B_2 in possible world w_1 is $\{w\ldots\}$
The extension of B_2 in possible world w_2 is $\{s\ldots\}$
The extension of A in possible world w_1 is $\{x\ldots\}$
The extension of A in possible world w_2 is $\{t\ldots\}$.

In this example, A (which is identical in this case with the closure of A) supervenes on the closure of B, but not on B, since x in w_1 and y in w_2 are indiscernible with respect to their B-properties but discernible with respect to their A-properties.

In sum, placing constraints on the nature of the sets when dealing with supervenience does not enable us to make all the supervenience claims that we would like to make and is quite unjustified.

1.4 Trivial Supervenience

The thesis of the supervenience of A on B is intended to provide an intermediate position between the view that the predicates of both sets are mutually independent, and the view that the predicates of A are reducible to the predicates of *B*. The concept of supervenience is therefore liable to two kinds of attacks: that it is too strong a relation, and hence entails reductionism; and that it is too weak a relation, and hence cannot guarantee determinacy. I deal with the first kind of criticism in the next chapter, and with the second kind in this section.

The notion of supervenience is supposed to give formal content to the following intuitions:

1. *A*-properties are determined by *B*-properties.[11]
2. *A*-properties are dependent on *B*-properties.
3. An object has *A*-properties in virtue of its having *B*-properties.
4. *B*-properties underlie *A*-properties (Blackburn, 1985:50).
5. *B*-properties realize *A*-properties.

Showing that a formal concept captures a particular intuition is obviously very difficult, and cannot be proven. However, it can be shown that counter-examples fail. Counter-examples of the kind I shall consider describe cases in which two sets of predicates, *A* and *B*, satisfy the formal definition of supervenience, yet intuitively we would not say that *A* is determined by *B* (or that it satisfies any of the other intuitions listed above). Of course, the fact that certain counter-examples fail does not guarantee that there are no sound counter-examples; I hope, however, that my treatment of the examples is general enough to show that a wide category of possible counter-examples can be refuted in a similar way.

Before going on, let me address a problem: I have offered five distinct definitions of supervenience. How can I claim that the formal definition of supervenience reflects a particular intuition without choosing one definition? My strategy at this point will be to show that the counter-examples fail to show that the strongest definition of supervenience—supervenience$_3$—does not satisfy our intuitions about supervenience.[12] As supervenience$_3$ is problematic, because of the ontological commitments it entails and the modal predicate calculus it involves, I will show that supervenience$_2$, and sometimes even supervenience$_1$, suffice for most of our needs.

I shall consider two families of counter-examples. The first attempts to show that in certain conditions the supervenience thesis is trivially true. In those conditions, the thesis is true even when *A* does not intuitively seem to be determined by *B*. The second family of examples includes cases in which the formal definitions of supervenience hold, yet *A* is independent of *B*. This category of examples distinguishes between dependence and determinacy.

The thesis of supervenience, recall, is formulated as a generalization: $(x)\ (y)\ (x =_b y \rightarrow x =_a y)$. By $x =_b y$ I mean that *x* and *y* share the same *B*-

properties. The supervenience thesis is trivially true when there are no discernible x and y such that $x =_b y$. This is the case when the B-predicates suffice to describe an object uniquely. In such cases, the law of the identity of indiscernibles holds, and the supervenience of A on B holds in virtue of it. This argument for the triviality of supervenience has been advanced by Currie (1991:248–249) and Miller (1991:695–701), among others.

One way of countering this argument is to constrain set B so that its predicates cannot describe an object uniquely. According to this answer, only intrinsic predicates, or only properties (and not relations), may be included in set B. As we have seen in section 1.2, such a constraint would make supervenience claims false in contexts where we want to say that there is determinacy. Hence, rather than choosing this answer, I will point out the flaws in the argument itself.

If the argument is valid, then examples such as the following should not satisfy the definitions of supervenience:

B = predicates that ascribe a time and place of birth to human beings.

A = predicates that ascribe moral properties to human beings.

In this example, the law of the identity of indiscernibles holds, and Currie's argument may therefore be used to deduce the supervenience of the moral properties of human beings on their time and place of birth. Yet intuitively we would not wish to say that the moral properties of human beings supervene on their time and place of birth.

This example, and many similar ones, can be countered thus: observe a person a and suppose that this person has changed with respect to moral properties. Specifically, he/she was a villain until December 31, 1992, and became a saint on January 1, 1993. Comparing a in 1993 with a in 1992, we will find a difference in A-properties but not in B-properties (a's time and place of birth have obviously not changed). Hence, supervenience does not hold in this example, since, as argued earlier, when supervenience$_4$ does not hold, neither does any other kind of supervenience.[13]

Thus, when dealing with the supervenience of properties that are not eternal (which is usually the case), the fact that the B-predicates suffice to describe an object uniquely does not trivialize the supervenience thesis. In such cases, the supervenience thesis provides information about the determination of A by B, because it poses constraints on the changes that an object may undergo with respect to the predicates of A.

From my answer, it is possible to deduce the cases in which the supervenience will be trivial—namely, when set A_I consists of eternal properties (i.e., properties with respect to which objects do not change); for example:

B = predicates that ascribe a time and place of birth to human beings.
A_I = predicates that ascribe a time and place of death to human beings.

Since the time and place of death of a particular human being do not change, A_I supervenes trivially on B. Thus, if we are not prepared to say that a human being's time and place of death are determined by the time and place of his or her birth, then we have a counter-example to the claim that supervenience captures the intuitive notion of determinacy.

There are two ways of countering these examples. First, we may say that in the example above, supervenience$_1$, supervenience$_2$ and supervenience$_4$ are trivially true, but supervenience$_3$ is false. Our person a, who was born at a certain time and place, could have died twenty years earlier than he/she actually did. This contradicts supervenience$_3$, since a in possible world w_I (in which he/she died twenty years earlier) and a in the actual world are indiscernible with respect to B-predicates, but discernible with respect to A-predicates.

The second way of countering the examples is to say that they are not relevant to discussions about supervenience, because such discussions usually deal with properties with respect to which objects can change: a once moral person may stop being so; a picture that was pretty can stop being pretty;[14] and a person may feel pain at a certain point in time and then stop feeling it. This strategy is appealing to those who find the notion of supervenience$_3$ problematic, because it shows that, in interesting contexts of discussion, the notions of supervenience that are weaker than supervenience$_3$ are also false where we would intuitively judge that there is no determinacy.

Note that I am not claiming that there are no cases in which the supervenience of a set of predicates A on a set of predicates B is trivial. My claim is only that coming up with such examples is more complicated than it seems at first sight. In particular, I have shown that incorporating into the set of base predicates predicates that describe an object uniquely does not suffice to make the supervenience trivial.

There is an additional criticism against the definition of supervenience, similar to the one presented above in that it is also based on the claim that the formal definitions are too weak and hence apply in cases in which we would not intuitively say that there was determinacy or dependence. Grimes (1991) discusses the following example: in a possible world w, there are two objects, x and y, which have exactly the same mental properties, but y has no physical properties. In this world, the mental supervenes on the physical: both supervenience$_1$ and supervenience$_4$ hold. Yet, according to Grimes, intuitively we would not wish to say that the mental is dependent on the physical, since:

> the mental seems in part to have a life of its own insofar as it has certain mental properties yet is entirely barren of any physical properties. (Grimes, 1991:81)

According to Grimes, this example shows that the formal definitions express determinacy but not dependence. In world *w*, the physical determines the mental, since a complete physical description of an object determines its mental properties; but the mental properties of an object are not dependent on its physical properties, since they may apply to an object that lacks physical properties altogether.

I disagree with Grimes. In my view, if we take a closer look at this example we will see that my definitions of supervenience express a strong notion that does not allow for complete independence between the mental and the physical. In Grimes' example, recall, object *y* has mental properties but no physical ones. If we assume that the mental properties supervene (in all the senses of the word) on the physical properties, we will reach strange conclusions about mental properties:

a. Let y_1 be a (different) possible object that has mental properties but lacks physical properties. From supervenience$_3$ it follows that y_1 and *y* are mentally indiscernible, i.e., have exactly the same mental properties. It follows hence that there can only be one mental type of objects that lack physical properties.

b. Owing to supervenience$_4$, *y* cannot change with respect to its mental properties; in other words, there is no mental property *M* that applies to *y* at *t* but not at t_1.

c. *y* has always and will always exist. Otherwise, there would be conflicts with global supervenience: the possible world in which *y* goes on to exist just after having stopped existing in *w* is physically indiscernible from *w*, but mentally discernible from it. Similar considerations lead to the conclusion that *y* exists in every possible world.

d. All the mental properties of *y* are necessary: *y* has the same properties in every possible world.

According to a–d, the combination of the thesis of the supervenience of the mental on the physical with the existence of an object that has only mental properties entails the conclusion that the mental properties of this object are eternal, necessary, and do not distinguish it from other objects. Surely, this is not the kind of properties that we refer to when we discuss the mind-body problem. The mental properties we discuss are properties such as "thinks about John", "wants water", and "feels pain". Such properties are contingent and time-dependent, and can apply to a person *x* without applying to a person *y*. In Grimes' example, the mental supervenes on the physical, but I for one do not know any mental property that satisfies all the constraints that follow from the example.

The general conclusion from my discussion of Grimes' example and Currie's argument is that, as far as mental properties that are contingent and time-dependent, and which distinguish between objects, are concerned, the definitions of supervenience do express determinacy and dependence.

1.5 Appendix: A Model-Theoretic Treatment of Supervenience

In my definitions of some of the notions of supervenience (supervenience$_2$, supervenience$_3$ and global supervenience), I have used modal concepts: I have quantified over possible worlds. One presupposition of such quantification is that the set of relevant possible worlds is given.

It is possible to define concepts that are similar to the modal concepts of supervenience without appealing to the notion of possible worlds: mathematical models can be used instead. I shall present a few of these definitions, and compare them to the modal definitions. My conclusion will be that these definitions present no philosophical advantage over the modal ones: they are as ontologically committed, and they too use the concept of possibility without analysing it. Their only advantage is that they can be used to provide a more precise proof of statements about the logical relations between the different notions of supervenience on the one hand and the concept of reduction on the other (as I show in Chapter Two).

Hellman and Thompson (1975:559) give the following definition of the global notion of supervenience: α is the set of models that represent scientific possibility. *A* and *B* are sets of predicates. We will say that truth in *B* determines truth in *A* iff for any two models *m* and *m'* that belong to α, if *m* and *m'* have the same *B*-truths, then *m* and *m'* have the same *A*-truths. This definition is, of course, reminiscent of the definition of global supervenience. Hellman and Thompson then proceed (p. 559) to define "reference in *B* determines reference in *A*" thus: for any two models *m* and *m'* that belong to α, if the interpretation of every predicate in *B* is identical in *m* and in *m'*, then the interpretation of every predicate in *A* is identical in *m* and in *m'*. This definition is closer to the definitions of local supervenience.

In order to understand the philosophical significance of these definitions, the nature of set α must be discussed. Hellman and Thompson present set α as "the set of models that represent scientific possibility" (p. 558). It is important to note that α is not an elementary set of models; it cannot, in other words, be defined as $\{m/m$ satisfies $T\}$ for a theory *T*. The reason for this is that the fact that a model *m* is elementarily equivalent to another model *m'*, which represents scientific possibility, does not in itself suffice to ensure that *m* too represents scientific possibility. This, in turn, results from the fact that we do not wish to treat every non-standard interpretation of *T* as representing possibility.[15]

The fact that α is not an elementary set has important consequences. If α were elementary, then:

a. The global notion defined by Hellman and Thompson would degenerate into the provability of every proposition in language *A* of *T* together with the propositions in language *B*.

b. The local notion would degenerate into definability.

Here is my proof of these two claims:

a. Suppose that $\alpha=\{m/m$ satisfies $T\}$, and suppose that truth in *B* determines truth in *A*.

I shall prove that every proposition in *A* can be proved from *T* together with the set of propositions in *B*.

Proof:

Suppose by negation that there exists a proposition *p* in language *A*, and that neither the proposition nor its negation are provable from *T* together with the set of propositions in *B*. It follows hence that the set $\{\sim p\}$ U *T* U {the set of propositions in *B*} is consistent, and so is the set $\{p\}$ U *T* U {the set of propositions in *A*}. Hence there is a model m that satisfies the first set, and there is a model *m'* that satisfies the second set. Both models belong to (and share the same theory *B*, but not the same theory *A*; and this contradicts the fact that truth in *B* determines truth in *A*.

b. Suppose that $\alpha=\{m/m$ satisfies $T\}$, and that reference in *B* determines reference in *A*. We want to prove that every predicate in *A* is definable by means of predicates in *B*. In other words, for every $A_i \varepsilon A$, there is a formula B^* which is formed out of the predicates in *B*, such that $m \varepsilon \alpha$ satisfies the sentence $(x)\ (A_i \leftrightarrow B^*x)$. The proof derives directly from Beth's theorem.

The upshot of this argument is that the set of models cannot be defined by means of a theory that is satisfied by all the models in *a*. Hence, the only way to understand the claim that the models in a represent scientific possibility is to say that the models in *a* represent possible worlds (in a scientific sense). The conceptual apparatus of the theory of models does not help us to make the distinction between a model that represents scientific possibility and other models, and therefore does not contribute more to the clarification of the concept of possibility than do the modal concepts. The conclusion hence is that there is no advantage to the statement that *a* is the set of all the models that represent scientific possibility over the statement that a is the set of all the possible worlds (in the scientific sense). I shall therefore assume that the set of models that is relevant to the definitions of Hellman and Thompson is identical to the set of possible worlds that is relevant to the definitions of supervenience. On the basis of this assumption, a precise comparison can be drawn between the definitions of supervenience and Hellman and Thompson's definitions.

a. The global supervenience of B on A is equivalent to the thesis that truth in B determines truth in A. This statement does not need to be proved, as the identity between the two concepts is a direct result of the identification of the set of models with the set of possible worlds.

b. If reference in B determines reference in A, then supervenience$_2$ is true.

Proof:

Suppose that $m \varepsilon \alpha$, $x \varepsilon m$ and $y \varepsilon m$ and that the same B-predicates apply to x and to y. Examine m', which is identical to m except that x replaces y. m' and m are identical with respect to the interpretation of the predicates in A. It follows hence that exactly the same A-predicates apply to x and to y: in other words, x and y are indiscernible with respect to A, and supervenience$_2$ is therefore true.[16]

c. If supervenience$_3$ is true, then reference in B determines reference in A.

Proof:

Suppose by negation that there is an m_l and an m_2 in α such that the interpretations of the predicates in B in m_l and in m_2 are identical, whereas the interpretations of the predicates in A are not. Hence, there exists an $a \varepsilon \alpha$ and an $A \varepsilon A$ such that a is part of the interpretation of A in m_l, but not of the interpretation of A in m_2. However, since the interpretations of the predicates in B in m_l and in m_2 are identical, a in m_l and a in m_2 are indiscernible with respect to the B-predicates. As a result of supervenience$_3$, they are indiscernible with respect to the A-predicates, and in particular with respect to the predicate A. This is a contradiction.

In sum, the model-theoretic definitions of determinacy provide a global concept that is exactly identical to global supervenience, and a local concept that is stronger than supervenience$_2$ and weaker than supervenience$_3$. As I cannot see that the concept of a model that represents scientific possibility has any advantage over the concept of possible world, I shall go on using the supervenience concepts defined by means of possible worlds. In the next chapter, however, I shall make an exception and use model-theoretic concepts in order to explain in an exact manner why the different notions of determinacy and supervenience do not imply reduction.

Notes

1 By the set of *B*-truths, I mean the set of all the true sentences in a language whose predicates are the predicates in *B*.

2 Nothing here hangs on whether supervenience is a relation between sets of predicates or between sets of properties.

3 If it is impossible for *x* to have a *B*-doppelganger, then supervenience$_2$* is trivially true. I discuss cases of trivial supervenience in section 1.4.

4 This description of Putnam and Burge's views cuts across the debate between them about the possibility of characterizing mental states, and thoughts in particular, independently of the physical and social environment. Putnam does so with the notion of "narrow psychological state", whereas Burge (1982) criticizes that notion.

5 See section 1.4.

6 I explain the tendency to mistakenly think that token-token identity guarantees local supervenience thus: a token-token identity thesis is usually taken to mean that any object that has an *A*-property also has a *B*-property. Obviously, such a thesis does not guarantee supervenience. Sometimes, however, a stronger thesis is meant by "identity thesis", namely, that any object *x* that has an *A*-property (A_l) also has a *B*-property (B_l) such that *x* is A_l *in virtue of* the fact that it is B_l, or that the property B_l *realizes* the property A_l. Under certain interpretations of the expressions "in virtue of" and "realizes", this addition to the identity thesis does indeed entail supervenience.

7 I count the case of an object that has undergone change with respect to *A* as a case in which there are two objects that are discernible with respect to *A*.

8 The appendix (section 1.5) may clarify the present discussion.

9 Van Cleve (1990:230) claims that closing *B* under negation may be problematic, as the negation of a physical predicate isn't necessarily a physical predicate. While it is true that negation does not preserve physicality, this fact is irrelevant to the question of the supervenience of the mental on the physical. Van Cleve's mistake results from the fact that he uses Kim's second definition of supervenience, under which it is not true that the supervenience of *A* on *B* is equivalent to the supervenience of the Boolean closure of *A* on the Boolean closure of *B*.

10 This claim is false when Kim's second definition of supervenience is used. It is possible for there to be two sets of predicates, *A* and *B*, such that the Boolean closure of *A* supervenes on the Boolean closure of *B*, but *A* does not supervene on *B*. The simplest instance of this is when *A* is defined as the Boolean closure of *B*.

11 I use the definitions of local supervenience here. The translation to global supervenience is obvious.

12 This is one of the reasons why David Lewis (1986:17) believes that supervenience$_3$ is the definition that corresponds to determinacy, and that all the other definitions should be abandoned.

13 I showed in section 1.1 that when supervenience$_4$ fails, so do supervenience$_1$, supervenience$_2$ and supervenience$_3$. In the example that I have just presented, the failure of supervenience$_4$ entails the failure of global supervenience as well. The reason for this is that the possible world in which a remains a villain does not differ from the world I have described with respect to *B*-predicates, but does with respect to *A*-predicates.

14 I am assuming that the individuation of a picture is the same as that of a physical object (rather than having special conditions of individuation as an work of art). Hence, the picture may stop being pretty if, for example, additional color is applied to it.

15 The interpretation of "cats" as cherries, for example, does not represent a scientific interpretation. See Putnam (1981:34); see also Teller (1983:142), on the relation between the notions of possibility and of standard interpretation.

16 This proof assumes that $m'\varepsilon\alpha$. On this assumption, if m represents scientific possibility, then so does any model that is arrived at by exchanging indiscernible elements (with respect to B). I cannot prove this assumption, as Hellman and Thompson do not pose any constraints on a. If the assumption is false, then it is possible to make up an example in which the determinacy of reference holds, and supervenience$_2$ does not.

2 Reduction

2.1 Introduction

In the preceding chapter we saw that the defined concepts of supervenience are strong enough to express an intuition of determinacy. In the present chapter, I aim to show that they are not, however, too strong; that is, they do not entail the possibility of a reduction of *A*-predicates to *B*-predicates.

The first section presents a general discussion of the concept of reduction and the motivations for offering reductionist theses. We shall see that these motivations impose restrictions on the nature of the set of predicates to which we reduce (the base-set). The base-set must include predicates which are suitable for a reduction, and therefore, as we shall see in the second section, this set cannot be closed under infinite conjunction and disjunction.

In the third section I will show that as a result of the above restrictions, reduction cannot be derived from supervenience, and that there is a coherent possibility of supervenience without reduction. In the fourth section I will illustrate why it is justified to expect that supervenience will hold in certain cases in which reduction is impossible.

In the fifth section I will show that even those few cases in which reduction is possible do not imply an anti-realist position. This will prepare the grounds for the main thesis of this work: that it is non-reductive supervenience, rather than reduction, that implies anti-realism.

2.2 What is Reduction?

According to Nagel, reduction is:

> the explanation of a theory or a set of experimental laws established in one area of inquiry, by a theory ... formulated for some other domain. (1961:538)

Nagel assumes that using theory *B* to explain theory *A* is, like any explanation, a derivation of theory *A* from theory *B*. A reduction becomes interesting and important when theory *A* includes theoretical terms that do not belong to theory *B*. In such a case, theory *A* cannot be deductively derived from theory *B*, unless we assume propositions which draw a connection between the terms in theory *A* and those in theory *B*. Such bridge laws need not formulate a necessary and sufficient condition in terms of theory *B* for every term in theory *A*. According to Hempel (1969:188), we use the law:

$$(x)\ (Q_1x \Rightarrow Q_2x)$$

in theory *B*, together with the bridge laws

$$(x)\ (R_1x \Rightarrow Q_1x)$$

$$(x)\ (Q_2x \Rightarrow R_2x)$$

to derive

$$(x)\ (R_1x \Rightarrow R_2x)$$

which belongs to theory *A*, despite the fact that the bridge laws do not supply a necessary and sufficient condition from *B* for the application of the *A*-predicates. The status of these bridge laws is in dispute. Nagel claims that they are not analytical statements and that they constitute a combination of conventions and empirical content (Nagel, 1961:356–7).

Nagel presents an accurate analysis of the concept of the reduction of theory *A* to theory *B*. He does not, however, provide an explanation of a reduction of *A*-properties to *B*-properties. Furthermore, he claims that the concept of reducing properties is "potentially misleading and generates spurious problems" (1961:364). If we do not anchor the set of *A* properties in theory *A* and the set of *B*-properties in theory *B*, he claims, the question whether the set of *A*-properties can be reduced to the set of *B*-properties is meaningless. The argument is as follows:

> the "natures" of things, and in particular of the "elementary constituents" of things, are not accessible to direct inspection ... Such "natures" must be stated as a theory and are not the objects of observation; (Ibid.)

In this light, the answer to the question "is the set of *A*-properties reducible to the set of *B*-properties?" depends on the theory in which set *A* is anchored, since we cannot know anything about the properties in *A* except through a theory. We have no way to ask whether the properties themselves, by virtue of their essence or their nature, can be reduced to *B*, since there is no "essence" or "nature" beyond the accepted theory. A different theory would attribute some other "nature" to the *A*-properties.

Hempel responded to this argument by claiming that while it is true that when we discuss the reduction of properties we relativize to a theory, we do so with respect to true theories rather than those that are accepted at present (p. 182). Thus Hempel (1968:182) defines reduction as follows: *A* can be reduced to *B* iff every true theory in language *A* is reducible to a true theory in language *B*.

One of the problems in Hempel's analysis is his reference to possible theories rather than existing ones. Such an analysis fails to provide ways to describe science as we know it. Furthermore, there may be changes in the store of terms pertaining to true theories. Thus the distinction between *A*-terms and *B*-terms may well disappear.

Hempel is aware of these problems, and claims that we are faced with the following dilemma: for the sake of clarity, a reductionist thesis can be expressed formally and relative to theories in which the terms are anchored (as done by Nagel), but if we do so, "we fail to express its philosophical intent" (Hempel, 1969:183). On the other hand, in order to express the ontological intuitions which motivate a reductionist thesis, such a thesis must be understood as expressing a relation between two sets of properties rather than a relation between theories, but then, "the resulting statement proves to be seriously obscure and elusive" (ibid.).

It follows that there are two possible motivations for a reductionist thesis. I will call the first a scientific motivation: the desire to explain in what sense one field of knowledge is more fundamental than another, and particularly, to determine whether there is a universal field of knowledge. The question of the unity of science belongs to this kind of motivation. I will call the second a philosophical motivation: the desire to explain in what sense a particular field of properties allows for an exhaustive description of different aspects of the world, whereas another field of properties is not necessary for a description of the world and is thus expendable. Nagel's analysis addresses the first motivation, whereas Hempel's attempts to address the second one as well. My aim in this chapter is to view supervenience as a relation between properties which constitutes an alternative to reduction. It is thus clear that I will address myself more to the second motivation. To this end, let us attempt to clarify the ontological intuition discussed by Hempel.

I do agree with Hempel's claim that a formulation attempting to express ontological intuitions will be vaguer than one which disregards such intuitions. The definition I will be using is: the set of properties $A = \{A_1, A_2...\}$ is reducible to the set of properties $B = \{B_1, B_2...\}$ if for every A_i that belongs to *A* there exists a particular combination B^* of properties in *B* such that (x) $(A_i x \Leftrightarrow B^* x)$.

The above definition follows that of definability in logic, and I will therefore alternate between the terms "reduction of *A* to *B*" and "definability of *A* by *B*".

It is important to note that my definition is independent of theories about *A* or *B*. According to it, the generalization $(x)\ (A_i x \Leftrightarrow B^* x)$ is true. The property "*p* is true" is independent of theory, unlike the properties "*p* is logically derived from *T*" and "*p* is confirmed by *T*".

I must therefore assume that although the expressions I am defining as well as those used in the definition are in some respects theoretical, they do not receive their meaning solely from the theories in which they are anchored. Since Nagel does not want to assume this, he does not use the concept of truth to define a reduction. Yet it is necessary to make use of this concept, as both Hempel and I have done in our definitions, if the possibility of reduction is to be made relevant to ontological questions such as:

> Are mental states nothing else than brain states? ... Are living organisms no more than complex physicochemical systems? (Hempel, 1969:179)

In light of this interest, I will explain why, in the context of this work, my own definition of reduction is preferable to Hempel's.

1. As I have mentioned, both my definition and Hempel's make use of a semantic concept of truth. But Hempel also makes use of the term "all true theories". This use generates problems which my own definition does not: (a) it is possible that a true theory in language *A* is reducible to a true theory in language *B* whereas another true theory in language *A* cannot be reduced to a true theory in language *B;* and (b) as was mentioned earlier, there is no guarantee that the terms used in all possible true theories will be divided into *A* and *B* terms as is the case at present.

2. Hempel's definition makes it necessary to ask whether the generalizations in language *A* are derived from those in language *B*, and it is thus relevant only to those sets of predicates in which generalizations obtain. But our interest in reduction is not confined only to these cases. Many philosophers argue that there are no generalizations in ethics and aesthetics. Others argue that there are none in psychology. In such cases, Hempel's definition collapses into my own.

3. A similar problem: both Hempel's and Nagel's definition assume that domain *A* is unproblematic as a field of knowledge: propositions (and generalizations) in domain *A* are as accessible to knowledge as those in domain *B*. But reductionist theses in philosophy arose precisely where a particular field of propositions was, for different reasons, viewed as problematic. Thus, a definition of reduction which assumes as little as possible as to the nature of domain *A* is preferable to our ends.

To conclude, I will emphasize that despite the ontological nature of my definition of reduction (ontological because it is not relative to a theory), it must comply with epistemological constraints. Hempel expresses this point when he says that an ontological reduction thesis is significant despite its vagueness because it can be viewed in the following way:

> overextensions of much more restricted and intelligible assertions concerning the reducibility of the concepts and principles of some particular scientific theory to those of another. (Hempel, 1969:187)

The epistemological constraints with which a "reduction of properties" must comply are similar to those which must be complied by a "reduction of theories". I will present some of these:

1. We use the properties in *A* and *B* to describe the world. (It follows from the thesis that *A* is reducible to *B* that we can describe the world using only *B*-properties.) We must therefore be able to understand these properties. Furthermore, *A*-properties must be meaningful even before the reduction (Nagel, 1961:352).

2. The propositions which define *A*-predicates by recourse to *B*-predicates are a particular case of bridge laws. Thus, like these laws, they must enable us to derive generalizations in *A* (to the extent that these exist), and to derive *A*-truths that we knew before the reduction.

3. The reducibility of *A* contradicts its autonomy. If *A* is an autonomous domain, then it is impossible to predict or explain *A*-phenomena (or at least, not all of these) by recourse to other terms. The autonomy of psychology, for example, is expressed by the fact that there exist psychological explanations for psychological phenomena which cannot be explained solely by physical theory. Even knowledge of the entire physical theory as well as the initial physical and psychological conditions does not enable the prediction of such psychological phenomena.

Reducing *A* to *B* cancels out this kind of autonomy, because it allows for the explanation (and prediction) of propositions in language *A* by recourse to the *B*-theory. Bridge laws must appear in such explanations, and for these laws to grant explanatory power to the derivation of the *A*-proposition, they cannot be random generalizations: they must be law-like.

We can conclude that not every generalization that links an *A*-predicate and a combination of *B*-predicates can operate as a bridge law in reduction, or as a definition of the *A*-predicate. The generalization must be law-like. This imposes restrictions on the type of predicate that appears in bridge laws. Let us call those that can "a predicate suitable for reduction". It follows that we cannot close the base set under all the mechanisms of predicate-formation. This is so because certain mechanisms do not preserve the property "being a predicate that is suitable for reduction". That is, from predicates that are suitable for reduction we may create unsuitable predicates by such mechanisms. In the following section, I will use this consideration to reject some of the proposals for certain closure constraints on set *B*.

2.3 Closure Constraints on the Sets of Predicates in Reduction

Interest in the concept of supervenience is predominantly due to that fact that it provides an alternative to other relations of determinacy between two sets of predicates. I will discuss two such relations: definability (or reduction), and entailment (or law-like relations). I am claiming that as opposed to supervenience, these concepts necessitate a restriction of the sets. In these cases, questions regarding the nature of the restriction, that is, under which operators the set should be closed, are fundamental.

I will begin by explaining why constraints on the nature of the sets under definability or entailment relations are required. Note that when we say, for example, that every *A*-predicate can be defined by recourse to *B*-predicates, we are claiming that there is a particular combination of *B*-predicates that is logically, conceptually, nomologically or materially equivalent to this predicate. If this claim is to be more than merely vacuously true, the combination of predicates must be given in some kind of structure. Not every open formula in which predicates from the set appear creates a predicate which is a member of the set: we will require that aside from the given predicates, only logical expressions appear in the formula. But in order to determine whether a particular expression is logical or not, we must determine what logic we are using. I will assume that we are using logic of the first order. In light of this assumption, supported by the discussion offered later in this section, the base sets will be closed under finite Boolean combinations, rather than other operators, such as infinite disjunction.

The need to restrict the means of expression does not come up only in the discussion of definitions. Such a restriction is also necessary in a discussion of laws or entailment relations. Among other things, a law is a proposition, and as such it must be expressed in language. This raises two questions: what language are we using and what mechanisms of predicate creation does it include. This is equivalent to the question of the nature of the sets. For example, if we allow the creation of new properties through the negation operator, we require the sets to be closed under negation. We must therefore determine what operators will be permitted when discussing definability and entailment relations.

In order to understand the arguments involved in rejecting certain operators, let us return to Bacon's law of diagonalization. I will show why we should not require that the sets be closed under this law, and will subsequently extract the general considerations which serve as guidelines for such rejections.

Note that set *B* is closed under the law of diagonalization iff:

> Where P_w is the extension of *P* at world *W* and $B_w = \{P_w/P$ belongs to $B\}$, *B* is also to contain any property *Q* such that Q_w belongs to B_w for each world *W*. (Bacon, 1986:65)

Bacon argues that sets *A* and *B* are closed under the diagonalization mechanism. Using this assumption, he derives equivalence between the different versions of supervenience, such as, for example, between supervenience$_2$ and supervenience$_3$. He also derives equivalence between the supervenience of *A* on *B* and the reducibility of *A* to *B*. These equivalences lead to the conclusion that the concept of supervenience does not add anything to that of reduction and is therefore superfluous. In order to preserve the difference between the concept of supervenience and that of reduction, as well as the difference between the versions of supervenience, I will show why Bacon's requirement that *B* will be closed under the mechanism of diagonalization is flawed.

In order for an *A*-predicate to be defined by *B*-predicates, or in order for us to be able to say that there is a law that connects them, it is not enough for the *A*-predicate to have the same extension as a predicate created by a diagonalization of *B*-predicates. Even identity of extensions in all possible worlds does not ensure law-likeness and definability. What is missing in these "diagonal" properties? Diagonal propositions are, in the formal sense, "properties": they are functions from possible worlds to sets of objects. But when this is the only justification for accepting properties, their number becomes inflated. The following are several characteristics of diagonal properties which disqualify them from forming the base for reduction:

1. We have no way of capturing them through their intension. That is, we have no concept which corresponds to a diagonal property. Such properties are generally not accessible to us.

2. They are not natural: there is no similarity between different objects which belong to the extension of a single diagonal property.

3. They cannot be projected.[1]

These characteristics correspond to those properties that Lewis has termed "abundant". In the following passage he discusses the distinction between *abundant* and *sparse* properties:

> There is another great rift in our talk of properties. Sometimes we conceive of properties as *abundant*, sometimes as *sparse*. The abundant properties may be as extrinsic, as gruesomely gerrymandered, as miscellaneously disjunctive, as you please. They pay no heed to the qualitative joints, but carve things up every which way. Sharing of them has nothing to do with similarity. Perfect duplicates share countless properties and fail to share countless others; things as different as can be imagined do exactly the same. The abundant properties far outrun the predicates of any language we could possibly possess. There is one of them for every condition we could write down, even if we could write at infinite length and even if we could name all those things that must remain nameless because they fall outside our acquaintance. In fact, the properties are as abundant as the sets themselves, because for any set whatever, there is the property of belonging to that set. It is these abundant properties, of course, that I have identified with the sets. (Lewis, 1986:59–60)

In order to understand the importance of characteristics 1–3, we must remember why it is that we are looking for laws and reductions. As we saw in the previous section, the claim that *A* is reducible to *B* expresses the attempt to lend scientific content to the intuition that there is nothing in the *A*-properties or *A*-phenomena beyond the *B*-properties or *B*-phenomena. According to Hempel, a reduction must fulfill two requirements. The first, that all *A*-predicates be defined by *B*-predicates, and the second, that all the phenomena in *A* (particularly laws) be explained by recourse to the laws of *B*. Hempel argues that such a definition is empirical, rather than analytical:

> It is expressed by empirical laws ... [it] depends on the extent to which suitable connecting laws can be established. (Hempel, 1966:104–105)

A reduction is not merely an identity of extensions (not even in all possible worlds): it is both more and less than that. I will focus on those aspects in which reduction amounts to more than a sharing of extensions. We have seen that reduction requires law-like connections—non-random generalizations. As we know, it is difficult to distinguish between laws and random generalizations. At this stage, however, it is sufficient to accept the position shared by Goodman (1983), Quine (1969) and Davidson (1982), that one of the factors influencing the categorization of a generalization as law-like or random is the type of predicate which appears in it. The third reservation, which shows that diagonal predicates cannot appear in laws, proves relevant in light of this claim.

The fact that it is reasonable to view reductionist positions as speculative theses on the development of science raises an additional objection to diagonal predicates. Thus, for example, Hempel argues the following regarding the relations between the domains of knowledge:

> In the course of further scientific research, biology will eventually come to be reduced to physics and chemistry. (Hempel, 1966:105–106)

Another version of this objection is the view of reductionist positions as methodological recommendations: we ought to look for laws which reduce *A*-phenomena to *B*-phenomena. In both versions, it is fundamental that predicates be projectible.

The epistemological constraints on reduction, raised in the previous section, strengthen the first and second reservations. These stated that *A*-properties and *B*-properties must be properties that we understand and can use to describe the world. According to the first reservation, we have no concept which corresponds to a diagonal predicate, and according to the second, a diagonal predicate does not describe an aspect of similarity; both reservations therefore show that we cannot use diagonal predicates to describe the world.

To my mind, there are many cases in which infinite Boolean combination are similar to Bacon's diagonal properties (in these respects). The first versions of behaviorism, for example, argue for the reduction of mental concepts to physical ones. I agree with Hempel's claim (1966:109) that it is hard to believe that there will be a concept different from "intelligence" that will apply to all intelligent behaviors. It thus follows that a mental property is not accessible to us by recourse to pure physical (or behavioral) concepts. If Hempel is correct, the infinite disjunction of all intelligent behaviors demonstrates the similarity between infinite Boolean combinations and diagonal properties. In this case, operators are used to create properties which are not suitable to ground laws, nor reduction therefore, from other properties which are suitable to such needs. In such contexts, we must therefore not require the sets to be closed under infinite Boolean combinations.

To conclude, when discussing connections of entailment and definability, sets *A* and *B* are closed under finite disjunction and conjunction, and under negation.[2] They are not closed under infinite disjunction and conjunction and certainly not under Bacon's diagonalization.

2.4 Supervenience does not Entail Reduction

The innovation in the concept of supervenience depends upon the possibility of there being a relation of determination between two sets of predicates, but not between the predicates taken singly. I will demonstrate this possibility in two stages. In the first stage, I will investigate the connection between the supervenience of *A* on *B* and the existence of entailment relations between *A*-predicates and *B*-predicates. In the second, I will investigate the connection between the supervenience of *A* on *B* and the possibility of defining *A*-predicates by *B*-predicates. In both cases, the conclusion is that the formal possibility exists. When discussing known predicates however, we can find cases of supervenience without definability, but I have not encountered any clear cases of supervenience without entailment relations.

2.4.1 *Supervenience and Entailment Relations*

Let us assume that there are entailment relations between *A*-predicates and *B*-predicates. In this way, for every A_i that belongs to *A*, there are combinations of predicates in *B* (B' and B^*) such that the following propositions are true:

$$(x)\ (B^*x \rightarrow A_i);\ (A_i \rightarrow B'x).$$

For these entailments to be laws, there are additional requirements, but I will not discuss them at this point. I will merely show that as long as we are only requiring truth, and even truth in all possible worlds, supervenience$_1$ is still not ensured (neither, therefore, are supervenience$_2$ and supervenience$_3$). Let us observe the following example:

B = {*x is a mother, x is a person*}; *A* = {*x is a woman*}.

There are, clearly, entailment relations between *A* and *B*. Every woman is a person and every mother is a woman. The concept "being a woman" does not, however, supervene in supervenience$_1$ on the properties "person" and "mother". This is because there could be a case in which there are two people who are not mothers, but the first is a woman and the second is a man. This shows us that the existence of entailment relations does not ensure supervenience$_1$, supervenience$_2$ or supervenience$_3$. These entailment relations also do not ensure supervenience$_4$, because a woman can stop being a woman without changing with respect to her properties in *B*. She/he will continue to be a person and not a mother, for example.[3]

There are also entailment relations which do entail supervenience. One of these is definability, which I will discuss later on. The second is exhaustive lawlikeness, which holds in cases such as the following: every *A*-predicate has a sufficient condition which is formulated by *B*-predicates; in addition, for every x, if x satisfies an A-predicate, x must fulfill one of these sufficient conditions. In cases in which such exhaustive lawlikeness holds in our world, supervenience$_1$ is ensured. If it holds in every possible world that belongs to W, supervenience$_2$ and supervenience$_3$ also obtain.

I will now return to the general case of lawlikeness, and show that in a strictly logical-formal respect, there is no entailment in the opposite direction. That is, one set of predicates may supervene on a second set, despite there being no entailment relations between them. Here is the proof:

Let us assume an infinite set of predicates $\{B_1 ... B_n ...\}$. C is a subset of $P(N)$ defined as follows: if a set of natural numbers is infinite, then and only then does the set belong to C. Let us assume that an object has property A iff the set of indexes of sets B that apply to it belongs to C. In such a case $\{A\}$ supervenes on $\{B_1 ... B_n ...\}$, although there is no true proposition which expresses entailment from A to a combination of predicates B_i.

Of course, this formal possibility does not ensure that, in our conceptual system, there exist familiar predicates in which such relations hold. It certainly does not ensure that there exist domains where; a: we can know of the existence of supervenience, and b: we do not discover any laws. I will later investigate domains for which it is justified to argue that this formal possibility is realized, that is, that supervenience obtains between two sets of predicates despite their being no entailment relations between the predicates in the sets.

2.4.2 *Supervenience and Definability (or Reduction)*

Reduction can be viewed as a particular case in which entailment relations hold. A is reduced to B iff every A-predicate can be defined by B-predicates. That is, for every predicate $A_i \in A$ there is a finite combination of B^* predicates from B, such that the proposition $(x)(A_i x \Leftrightarrow B^* x)$ is true. As we saw in the previous sections, it is not sufficient in a reductionist thesis for these propositions to be true. They must be law-like generalizations and include predicates that are accessible to us.

Let us assume that all the A-predicates can be defined by B-predicates. Does A supervene on B? When the defining propositions have no modal power, that is, they are contingent, the supervenience that obtains is also contingent, that is, supervenience$_1$. However, when the defining propositions are true in the set of all possible worlds of a certain type, supervenience$_2$ and supervenience$_3$ hold relative to those possible worlds. This is the proof: Let us assume that in every possible world of a particular type the extension of A_i is equivalent to that of the corresponding B_j. Let us observe two possible objects that are indiscernible with respect to the *B*-predicates; I will show that they are also indiscernible with respect to the *A*-predicates. If, for example, B_i were true of the first object but not of the second, then for some j, A_j would also be true of the first object but not of the second; this contradicts the assumption that the two objects are indiscernible with respect to *A*.

Regarding supervenience$_4$, the consideration is somewhat different: if x changed with respect to an *A*-predicate, then as a result of definability, other *B*-properties hold, and thus x also changed with respect to *B*.

Hence, definability entails supervenience.[4] If entailment also holds in the opposite direction, then the concept of supervenience is the same as the concept of definability, and we have not added anything by introducing it. Thus the important question is whether supervenience is possible without definability. Before discussing examples of this, I will reject a general argument (Kim, 1984:170) which attempts to derive definability from supervenience.

Let us assume that supervenience$_1$ holds. Each of the objects in the extension of A_i will be characterized with respect to the *B*-predicates. That is, the first object in A_i is characterized by the conjunction of all *B*-predicates that apply to it. Let us signify this characterization as B^*_1, the second object as B^*_2, etc. The disjunction of all these characterizations, argues Kim, is the definition of A_i.

This proof has two faults. The first is that when the extension of A_i is infinite, the definition can only be expressed by an infinite disjunction. The second is that if *B* has an infinite number of predicates, we will need to use infinite conjunction to express B^*_1. Thus, as long as we limit ourselves to expressions of first order logic, a construction of the defining propositions is not possible. Note that when discussing supervenience$_2$ or supervenience$_3$, the problem is aggravated. We may then want to say that the definition is true in all relevant possible worlds. Even when these definitions could be expressed (for example, when the number of predicates and objects is finite), the defining proposition will be true only in our world. For the proposition to be true in all possible worlds, it must be an infinite disjunction. This is the case because even when there is a finite number of objects of a particular kind, the number of possible objects of this kind is infinite.

The following is a formal example of a description of two sets of predicates in which all versions of supervenience hold without there being definability. Let us assume that the following connection exists between the *B*-predicates and the *A*-predicates: the extension of A_1 is equal to the union of the extensions of all B_i. The extension of A_2 is equal to the union of the extensions of all B_i for even *i*s. The extension of A_n is equal to the union of the extensions of all B_is for every *i* that is a multiple of *n*. In this description A_1 is not defined by

B-predicates since these connections cannot be stated in sentences in first order language. Thus *A*-predicates are not definable by *B*-predicates. If the above connection between *B* and *A* holds in our world, we have supervenience$_1$. If the connection holds in all relevant possible worlds, we have supervenience$_2$, supervenience$_3$ and supervenience$_4$. This example thus shows that even the strictest concept of supervenience can hold without definability.

The fundamental reason that supervenience can hold without reduction is that the concept of supervenience is strictly ontological, whereas that of reduction is subject to epistemological constraints. The question whether the set of *A*-predicates supervenes on the set of *B*-predicates is solely dependent on predicates from the two sets. Reducibility, however, though not dependent on accepted theory (as argued by Nagel), is dependent on our ability to create theories. The limitations of our language are relevant to the concept of reduction, but not to the concept of supervenience. I will demonstrate this: phenomenalists argue that the language of material objects can be reduced to that of sense data. They may be right when subjunctive conditionals are included in the language of sense data. But they are clearly wrong if the language does not have a system which creates subjunctive conditionals (Dummett, 1982:78–79).

This difference between supervenience and reduction is formally expressed in the model theory treatment of supervenience. The determinacy of reference of *A* by *B* entails, according to the Beth theorem, the definability of *A*-predicates by *B*-predicates. But such entailment holds iff α is an elementary set of models, that is, a set of models that satisfy a particular theory. It thus follows that when *A* is reducible to *B*, a theory necessarily exists which characterizes all the relevant models. The existence of such a theory is, of course, dependent on the allowed systems of expression. When *A* supervenes on *B* however, a theory which characterizes α does not necessarily exist. The dependence of supervenience on our systems of expression follows from this (Hellman & Thompson, 1975:563).

Let us now turn to two examples of supervenience without definability. Unlike the artificial predicates constructed in the previous examples, these will employ familiar concepts.

1. *The Example of the Clock—McGinn*

> [T]he attribute of being a clock does not have a physical nature ... but it is still true that if two objects are physically indiscernible and one of them is a clock, then so is the other. (McGinn, 1982:30)

The claim is that the set of predicates $A = \{x \text{ is not a watch}, x \text{ is a watch}\}$ supervenes on the set of all physical predicates (we will call it B), although we cannot define all the A-predicates by recourse to B-predicates. Since we need not assume that B exhausts all physical predicates, there is no need to confound ourselves with the question which predicates are included in set B in order to understand this example. Let us assume that set B includes properties such as shape, weight, color, material the object is made of and so forth. Properties which characterize location in space-time will be left out in order to avoid rendering some of the propositions uninformative.

There are two intuitions in this supervenience claim. The first is that if two objects are physical duplicates, identical with respect to appearance and behavior, one cannot be a clock if the other is not. This is so since an object is a clock by virtue of its physical properties. The second intuition is that if a particular clock stops being one, it will be the result of some physical change: its hands have disappeared, its internal mechanism is beyond repair, and so forth.

The first intuition can be challenged by saying that an object's physical properties do not, by themselves, determine its being a clock. We must also consider the way it is used, or the purpose for which it was produced. It is thus possible to have two objects which are physical duplicates where one is a clock and the other is not; if, say, only one of them is being used as a clock, or if one was produced in order to indicate the time while the other was not. This poses a fundamental contradiction to supervenience: a contradiction which cannot be solved by claiming that supervenience is global and not local. This is the case since the external characterizations addressed by supervenience—the use and purpose of the object—are not physical.[5] We shall see that this is a highly relevant kind of objection to claims of supervenience: it argues that in order to determine the A-properties of an object, the subject who uses it, sees it, judges it, etc., must be considered.

In this case, however, the objection can be countered. Our use of the word clock does not justify such claims as: "*x* stopped being a clock because it was no longer being used to tell time". Our use of the word clock is related to the object's potential to tell time, and to its similarity to other objects that tell time or which are used to this end. Furthermore, if two objects only differ in that one was produced to be a clock and the other was produced for some other purpose and this difference is not expressed in the physical history of the two objects, then if we call the first a clock we will call the second one a clock as well.

Having removed this objection, the question of supervenience can be thus formulated: given two physically identical objects, is it possible that one can tell time while the other cannot? McGinn assumes a negative answer to this question. Assuming he is correct, this example indeed proves the coherence of supervenience without definability. This is so since the wide range (physically speaking) of actual and potential clocks does not allow us to formulate a definition of "clock" by recourse to physical terms alone.

2. *The Concept of Truth—Davidson*

Let us assume that *L* is a first order language, which is rich enough to express its syntax. The *B*-predicates are all the predicates of *L*. Davidson argues that set *A*, made up of the predicate "*x* is a true sentence in *L*" supervenes on *B*. This is so since in every possible world where two sentences have identical syntactical characteristics, their truth values are also identical.

The example requires clarification. The sentence "it is raining" is syntactically identical to itself, but while it is true at one time, it is false at another. This contradicts supervenience$_4$, and therefore all the other versions of supervenience. There are two ways to preserve supervenience in this example. One is to change the set of *A*-predicates to {*x is true at t, x is true at* t_1, *etc.*}. This solution is complicated: it requires us to consider other indexes, since the truth value of the sentence "I am tired", for example, changes at t in accordance with who is speaking, even though the syntax remains fixed. Furthermore, this calls for a definition of truth for indexical sentences. This problem requires separate treatment. For the purpose of the present argument, supervenience can be preserved in another way: it is sufficient to show that the given relation of determinacy holds in a more restricted domain of sentences; those that are eternal. That is, sentences whose truth value is independent of any aspect of the context in which they were uttered.

It is also necessary to clarify what is meant by a syntactic description of a sentence. The sentences "Joe is fat" and "Ruth is thin" do not have the same syntactical characterization. While their syntactical structure is identical, the syntactical description of the first is "the appearance of the single-place predicate 'fat' after that of the proper name 'Joe'". This description is not true of the second sentence. This is what is meant by the claim that the two sentences are syntactically different.

Having clarified these two points, we are ready to investigate which versions of supervenience hold in this example. *A* supervenes on *B* in supervenience$_1$ and supervenience$_2$. *A* does not supervene on *B* in supervenience$_3$ since the eternal sentence "the sun rises every day in Israel" is false in one possible world and true in another, with no syntactical change. Supervenience$_4$ holds, since the truth value of eternal sentences cannot change.[6]

According to Tarski's theorem, *A*-predicates cannot be defined by *B*-predicates. Entailment relations, however, exist between the two types of predicates. For example: "if a sentence has the form $pv \sim p$ then it is true". Davidson made use of this example in order to show that the concept of supervenience is coherent without laws. The above entailment relation shows that he failed to do so. Despite this weakness however, the example is interesting because it deals with familiar predicates and not merely ones that are formally possible.

Let us investigate the source and justification of the claim of supervenience in this example. Why do we think that truth supervenes on syntactical predicates? One answer is that this is a case of trivial supervenience. We know that the supervenience of *A* on *B* is uninformative when the indiscernible objects in *B* are simply identical; because of Liebnitz's law, identical objects converge in all their eternal properties (those that do not change over time), particularly in those properties that are expressed by the *A*-predicates. This answer draws our attention to the fact that the domain of our discussion includes only eternal sentences; those whose truth value depends only on their sentence-type. We can thus say that the objects in this domain are sentence-types. Such objects are only determined by their syntactical properties; that is, when their syntactical descriptions are identical, so are the objects. Thus all of their eternal properties are identical, particularly their truth value.

According to the second answer to the question of the source of supervenience in this example, the supervenience is not trivial. According to this answer, truth should be seen as a property of tokens or utterances, not sentence-types. We must therefore assume that belonging to a particular sentence-type rather than another is a property of the utterance itself. The supervenience is not trivial because the fact that two utterances have the same syntactical structure does not ensure that they are identical. The claim of supervenience ensures that in such a case, despite the difference of the utterances, they will have the same truth value. What is the explanation and the source of this supervenience? To my mind, the answer to this can be found in Tarski's definition of truth. Given a world, or a model, every stage in the recursion depends only on the syntax of the sentence for which truth is defined.

To conclude: formally speaking, all versions of supervenience can hold without definability or entailment relations. When discussing familiar predicates, supervenience$_1$ and supervenience$_2$ can obtain without definability, as was shown by Davidson's example. The example of the clock shows that all versions hold without definability or entailment relations. Davidson's example is preferable to the example of the clock since the undefinability of the *A*-predicates by the *B*-predicates can be proved.

2.5 Arguments against Reduction

In the previous sections I showed that supervenience is a weaker concept than reduction. The question is whether there is philosophical value to such a concept. Much of the present work deals with answering this question in the affirmative. In the present section I will show why we are justified in having such expectations of the concept of supervenience. To do this, I will present several types of arguments for the impossibility of reducing *A* to *B*, showing that even when such arguments are valid and grounded, they do not prove that *A* does not supervene on *B*.

2.5.1 *Multiple Realizability*

Fodor (1974) and Putnam (1975:291–303) have argued against the possibility of reducing the mental to the physical in the following way: every mental predicate can be realized by physical objects that are completely different. That is, given a mental predicate *M*, though the objects in its extension are physical, they need not have any common physical properties whatsoever. There is therefore no physical property that can constitute a definition of *M*.

There are different versions of this argument. They differ in the way they argue the move from multiple realizability to the claim that there is no physical property that can constitute a definition of *M*. All these versions reasonably assume that "physical property" denotes a property in the narrow sense: not every set of physical objects is characterized by a physical property.[7]

Fodor has grounded this move in a "probabilistic" consideration: a physical property is only suitable for reduction if it delineates a natural physical type. A natural physical type is one which appears in physical laws. Relative to the number of physical sets (that is, sets whose members are physical objects), there are few natural physical types. Given a set that was selected by a natural mental type, for completely different purposes than the need to detect physical laws, it is not probable that the set will also be characterized by a natural physical type. Fodor emphasizes that this argument is not conclusive, and does not necessarily indicate that there is no suitable natural physical type. The argument merely shows why it is probable that such a type will not be found.

The move from multiple realizability to the claim that there is no physical predicate that can define *M* can be justified by another consideration: a predicate only indicates a natural type if all the objects in its extension are similar to each other. More specifically, objects in an extension of a *physical* natural type must be *physically* similar to each other. Since there are objects that are not necessarily physically similar in the extension of a mental predicate, there is no physical natural type that unites all the *M*-objects. *M* cannot, therefore, be defined in physical terms.

In Putnam's version, the move is justified in a somewhat different way. Putnam reasonably assumes the following: the application of a physical predicate to an object depends on what the object is made of, or of what material it is comprised. But functional terms, such as "*x* believes that *p*" can apply to objects that are made of completely different materials, just as a single computer program can be operated by physical systems and materials that are completely different.

Even if these arguments are valid, we can see that they do not contradict the *supervenience* of the mental on the physical: let us assume that the mental supervenes on the physical. We can therefore deduce that for every mental predicate *M* there is an infinite disjunction of conjunctions of physical predicates *P*, such that *P* and *M* have equal extensions. This conclusion clearly does not contradict multiple realizability, since *P* need not be a physical natural type. Although the fact that an *A*-predicate is realized by objects that are completely different with respect to *B* contradicts the reduction of *A* to *B*, it does not contradict the supervenience of *A* on *B*.

2.5.2 *Holism*

According to Quine and Davidson, holism is the main reason that domain *A* cannot be reduced to domain *B:* this comes up in Quine's argument against the reduction of theoretical to observational claims (1953), and in Davidson's argument against psychophysical reduction (1982). One of the reasons these arguments are difficult to characterize is that the holism thesis can be understood in many ways. Let us interpret the holism of domain *A* in the following way: the significance of an *A*-proposition is determined by its entailment relations with all the other *A*-propositions, thus the truth value of a particular claim *a* depends on the truth values of all the other *A*-claims. In light of this interpretation, the argument from holism to irreducibility can be presented as follows: if *A* is reducible to *B*, then there is a *B*-claim *(b)* which is true iff *a* is true. It follows that we can know if *a* is true without considering other *A*-claims that are conceptually linked with *a*. However, to ignore the conceptual connections between *a* and other claims contradicts the holistic claim that *a*'s significance is determined by such connections.

Blackburn has summarized the argument as follows:

> These multifarious connections, these interanimations in a web of belief, mean that no one individual statement, considered in isolation, will be wholly identified through any purely downward anchoring in a different (*B*) vocabulary. (Blackburn, 1984:159)

I do not find this argument valid. It does not show that it is impossible to reduce a holistic claim *A* to *B*. It does, however, point to two important conclusions regarding such a reduction. The first—that if a holistic domain *A* is reduced to *B*, we cannot make an isolated check whether the reduction is correct. In other words, in order to check whether sentence *b* is the correct "translation" of sentence *a*, we must also check the translations of other sentences. I will sharpen this: let us assume that there is a conceptual connection between *a* and a^*, which ensures that we can deduce *a* from a^*. Let us also assume that the translation of *a* is *b*, and that the translation of a^* is b^*. If we cannot deduce *b* from b^*, then the reduction is not valid. The argument has so far shown us, therefore, that we must check the reduction globally, but not that reduction is impossible. It also shows that for *A* to be reduced to *B*, domain *B* must be at least as holistic as domain *A*.[8] Although both of these results are important, they do not show that holism does not allow reduction.

The following is an additional argument from holism against reduction. We can infer from the holism of *A* that it is impossible to verify the truth of an isolated claim in *A*. Rather, the complete *A* theory must be compared with the evidence. In important cases in which the *B*-claims describe the possible evidence, the truth value of claim *A* is determined by all the *B*-claims. (This, for example, is described in Two Dogmas: *B* is the collection of observational claims, and *A* is the collection of theoretical claims.) In such a case there is no reduction of *A* to *B:* based on the considerations presented earlier, an infinite collection of *B*-claims is not a *B*-claim which can be used as a suitable basis for reduction.

2.5.3. *Defeasibility*

The argument that defeasibility counters the possibility of reduction is similar to our previous argument. It runs as follows: according to the claim that domain *A* is defeasible, given the justification of claim *a* in *A* by claim *b* in *B*, there will always be a claim b_1 in *B* such that $b\&b_1$ justifies the negation of *a*. In such a case it is impossible to translate *a* into a particular *B*-claim.

It can, however, be translated into an infinite conjunction of *B*-claims, but such a conjunction is not itself a *B*-claim.

The above arguments to anti-reductionism from holism and from defeasibility are not arguments against the supervenience of *A* on *B*. I am not claiming that they prove the supervenience of *A* on *B*; merely that there is no contradiction between the holism of *A* and the supervenience of *A* on *B*. This is so because supervenience is precisely the claim that domain *A* is fully determined by the entire domain *B*, without there being an isolated predicate in domain *A* which is determined by one in domain *B*.

2.5.4. *The Problem of Status*

Reduction is occasionally offered as a solution to a difficulty caused by claims in domain *A*. Claims in *A* may have, in some of cases, undesirable ontological conclusions (such as the existence of values in a world). Furthermore, claims in domain *A* may give rise to epistemological problems (for example, because they cannot be known directly but only through the mediation of other claims). A reduction of *A*-claims to (unproblematic) *B*-claims should solve these problems by showing that the ontological and epistemological status of *A*-claims is identical to that of *B*-claims.

The following dilemma shows that reduction does not necessarily solve these problems: if the reduction is semantic, that is, the *A*-claim and the corresponding *B*-claim have the same meaning, then it is not clear how the *A*-claim entails problematic conclusions that do not follow from the equivalent *B*-claim. On the other hand, if the connecting principle is empirical, it is not clear how it can be known. According to this principle, *x* is *a* iff *x* is *b;* but in order to know that *x* is *a* we must discover that it is *b,* thus we will never be able to empirically discover the truth of the equivalence.

The fact that connecting principles are interpreted as identity claims creates other problems regarding their status. These problems are well known, so I will not discuss them here.[9] Arguments based on the problem of status that reject the possibility of reduction are not valid arguments against supervenience. This is the case because a supervenience thesis is not at all committed to the existence of connecting principles, and therefore does not create any problems regarding their status.[10]

2.5.5. *Dummett's Objection*

> It is impossible to introduce a vocabulary adequate for expressing statements of the reductive class without thereby introducing one adequate for the expression of statements of the given class. (Dummett, 1982:71)

This is a generalization of a classic objection to phenomenalism, which argues that claims about sense data cannot be formulated without using the language of material objects. Note that this objection is only relevant for cases in which the reduction of *A* to *B* aims to *explain* the meaning of sentence *A* by recourse to the corresponding *B* sentence. That is, cases in which reductionism is used as a claim that an *A*-sentence cannot be understood without understanding its corresponding *B*-sentence.

A supervenience thesis of *A* on *B*, however, is not committed to the semantic priority of *B*, that is, to an understanding of *A* claims by recourse to *B* claims. Thus such an objection does no harm to the supervenience thesis of *A* on *B*.[11]

I have thus far shown that supervenience is a weaker concept than that of reduction, and that even when a reduction of *A* to *B* is impossible, set *A* can supervene on set *B*. Furthermore, we have seen that the most important arguments against the possibility of a reduction of *A* to *B* do not show that *A* does not supervene on *B*. We will soon see that in the ethical and mental domains, in which reduction is not possible (some of the reasons for this were already mentioned in the previous section), supervenience of *A* on *B* does hold.

Before discussing these domains, let us investigate another general question. A reduction of *A* to *B* serves ontological interests as well. For example, if mental properties are reducible to behavioral ones, there are, in fact, no mental properties; if tables can be reduced to sense data, then there are in fact no tables in the world. In the following section, which concludes the general discussion of reduction, I will give a more critical treatment of this anti-realist motivation for reduction.

2.6 Realism and Reductionism

In order to investigate the connection between realism and reductionism, let us clarify what we mean by realism. Two metaphors are used as a basis for the discussion of realism. According to the first, the realist claims that the world (which we discover) exists independently of us, whereas the anti-realist claims that the world does depend on us and in a certain sense is created by us. In the second, the realist's view is that our claims describe (or at least, are able to describe) reality as it is, while the anti-realist claims that we project our needs and interests onto reality, and we can only describe it, via these needs and interests. Hume described the connection between the two metaphors as follows:

> The one discovers objects as they really stand in nature, without addition or diminution; the other has a productive faculty, and gilding or staining all natural objects with the colors, borrowed from internal sentiment, raises in a manner a new creation. (Hume, 1975 [1777]:294)

There are a great many theses which term themselves realistic.[12] Let us focus on that family of theses which clarify, to my mind, the basic metaphor of discovery/creation and that of naked/clothed reality. These two metaphors give expression to a facet which we will make use of to characterize realism: the claim of reality's independence of man. I accept Sober's two requirements of realism (1982:369):

(i) Realism is a declaration of independence
(ii) Man is not the measure of all things.

The realistic claim that truth is independent of us is still open to numerous interpretations. The particular domain of which truth is independent must be determined: is it independent of our mental state, our present knowledge or our fundamental capacity for knowledge? Furthermore, the kind of dependence that realism negates must be explained: is it logical, conceptual or causal dependence?

Let us opt for a characterization of realism as a thesis negating that truth is conceptually dependent on our capacity for knowledge. That is, the domain of which truth is independent is our capacity for knowledge and the negated dependence is conceptual. The realist claims that truth is independent of our capacity for knowledge, whereas the anti-realist argues that a claim is true iff it is justified under ideal conditions.

By "ideal conditions" we mean the state in which the believer is rational and has access to all the evidence. Putnam writes:

> 'Epistemically ideal conditions', of course, are like 'frictionless planes': we cannot really attain epistemically ideal conditions ... But frictionless planes cannot really be attained either, and yet talk of frictionless planes has 'cash value' because we can approximate them to a very high degree of approximation. (Putnam, 1981:55)

Just as our ability to approximate a frictionless plane lends content to idealization, so does our ability to approximate a state in which all the evidence is accessible to us. We understand an ideal state when we understand what is involved in approximating such a state. It is not difficult to understand what an approximation to an epistemically ideal state would be. Such an approximation can be arrived at in two ways: the first is to add evidence, and the second—to correct an error in the application of our epistemic norms. It thus follows that the only significance an anti-realist is willing to grant a particular error of judgment on my part is that it can be corrected—either by pointing my attention to additional evidence or to my irrationality. According to the realist, on the other hand, I am mistaken in a particular judgment if I am not reflecting reality as it is, even if, in principle, there is no way of showing me that I am mistaken.

The above captures both Putnam's modal characterization of realism (1983:21, 84) and Dummett's characterization (1978:146), although neither of these entail one another. Putnam says that a realist position is committed to the possibility of error. That is, even in a ideal state, in which all of the evidence for α is available to us, and we are completely justified in claiming α, we are still possibly mistaken. According to Dummett, the realist claims that even in an epistemically ideal state, we can be completely ignorant as to the truth value of α.

Note that my suggested characterization presents realism as a metaphysical position rather than an epistemological one. The fundamental opposition is between metaphysical and scientific realism. The former is committed to a non-epistemic definition of the truth, or at least to the fact that an epistemic definition is impossible. Scientific realism, however, relates to science and its development. Different versions of scientific realism range from a position by which our scientific propositions are for the most part true to one which holds that when scientists work in a rational way, science approaches truth.

Scientific and metaphysical realism do not entail one another, and further, tension exists between the two. It is easy for the metaphysical anti-realist, who identifies truth with ideal theory, to be a scientific realist. For him or her, truth is closely bound to our procedures of knowledge; thus, if we adhere to our epistemic norms, given a bit of luck, we will arrive at truth. This is Peirce's position. The metaphysical realist, on the other hand, who fully severs the concept of truth from our epistemic standards, renders truth far less accessible to us. This is Van Fraassen's position.

Unless another version is explicitly specified, all subsequent discussions of the problem of realism will refer to this version of realism, which claims that truth is not identical to ideal justification. This is the version used in many discussions of the issue[13] and it expresses, to my mind, the metaphor of creation. There is a two-way connection between the characterization of anti-realism according to this version and the metaphor of creation. The first direction is that if we create truth, rather than discovering a truth independent of us, our position is similar to that of the novelist. Novelists know the truths in their novel better than they know truths which they did not create. Hence, the anti-realist connection between truth and knowledge. The second direction is that if truth is identical to ideal justification, there is a sense in which it can be claimed that we create truth: according to this version, what makes a statement true is our acceptance of it under ideal conditions. That is, under such conditions it is justified according to our standards. We must therefore ask whether our standards are correct. The realist will argue that they are true iff using them will give us a closer approximation of truth. The anti-realist cannot use this definition as to the correctness of our standards, since truth was defined by these very standards. He will argue that there is nothing outside of us that will render these standards true: they are true because they are ours. We create the standards, truth is determined according to them, and it is in this sense that we create the truth.

This characterization of realism is generally discussed in a local sense. By 'a local discussion of realism', I refer to one which focuses on a particular set of propositions, and asks whether the concept of truth with respect to these propositions transcends our knowledge. The global discussion, by contrast, is not restricted to a given set of propositions, but attempts to see whether truth is always cut off from our ability to know it. A choice of the local discussion can be justified in two ways. The first, by claiming that there is no reason to assume that the answer to the question of the connection between truth and knowledge will be identical in all domains (Dummett, 1978:xxxi). We may be inventing the truths of mathematics, but discovering those of physics. The second is to say that our ability to formulate a coherent, global realist position (or an anti-realist one) is disputable (Sober, 1982).

Since the characterization of realism is local, we must ask which is the correct approach to truth with respect to a specific set of propositions: is it one which transcends our knowledge capacity? When we apply the above characterization of realism to a particular set of propositions, we arrive at a local characterization of realism:

> the belief that statements of the disputed class possess an objective truth value, independently of our means of knowing it: they are true or false in virtue of a reality existing independently of us. (Dummett, 1978:146)

Let us now investigate the connection between this characterization of realism and the possibility of reducing *A*-claims.[14] (Set *A* is the disputed class discussed by Dummett.) Let us focus on the following question: does a reductionist thesis with respect to *A* require an anti-realist approach to *A*?

Let us begin by refining this question. In the first place, reduction, as we have defined it, is a relation between two sets of predicates. *A*-predicates are defined by *B*-predicates. The question of realism, however, regards the status of propositions rather than predicates. It would thus be more accurate to present the question of the connection between reduction and realism as follows: Is an anti-realist thesis with respect to the set of propositions formulated in first order language with *A*-predicates entailed by the reduction of *A*-predicates to *B*-predicates?

Second, when searching for this connection, we are confronted by the problem that only one set of propositions is mentioned in the characterization of realism, whereas in that of reduction, two sets are mentioned: propositions of set *A* are reduced to those of set *B*. If a reductionist thesis with respect to *A* means that *A* is reducible to some set *B*, we clearly cannot infer anything regarding the question of realism from the possibility of reduction. This is so since every set of propositions is reducible to itself and this entails nothing about the "reality" of the set. A less trivial example is that even if the set of mental predicates is reduced to the set of neurophysical predicates, this does not entail an anti-realist conclusion regarding mental predicates (see Dummett, 1982:74). In sum, the fact that a set *A* is reducible to *some* set of predicates does not bear any significance to the question of realism about *A*. I will now show that in many discussions of realism a specific additional set of propositions is involved. As we know, according to Dummett's characterization, both realist and anti-realist agree that the following question must be addressed: in virtue of what is a proposition in set *A* true? They do not, however, agree on the answer to this question. The realist claims it is true in virtue of the fact that its truth conditions obtain—though it is not always possible to know whether they do. The anti-realist claims that a proposition in set *A* is true by virtue of conditions that we can, in principle, identify.

In light of this description of the argument on realism with respect to set *A*, I will present a set *B* of propositions relevant to the discussion: set *B* is composed of propositions which describe all the possible evidence to *A*-propositions.[15,16] This set is relevant to the discussion since the realist would say that in certain cases, a proposition in *A* can obtain even when none of the propositions in *B* which constitute evidence for it obtain. This is a case in which a proposition remains outside our capacity for knowledge. The anti-realist, however, would claim that an *A* proposition is true by virtue of a *B* proposition.

Let us use an example to explain the nature of set *B*. When *A* is a set of propositions that attribute mental states to other people, both realist and anti-realist will agree to the claim that only behavior constitutes evidence for *A* propositions. They will also agree to the claim that all possible behaviors can be described by sentences. Set *B* will be composed of these sentences. A realist with respect to mental states would say that there are cases in which α which belongs to *A* is true despite the fact that all the sentences in *B* that can be evidence for α are false, and thus the truth conditions for α will not be formulated solely by sentences from *B*. The anti-realist, on the other hand, will say that in these cases α cannot be true since the truth conditions for α are formulated by using *only* sentences from *B* which constitute evidence for α. The set of *B*-predicates is the set of predicates that appear in evidence-sentences for *A*.

We can now formulate the question more accurately: is anti-realism with respect to *A* entailed by a reduction of *A*-predicates to predicates that appear in evidence sentences for *A*?

Let us first answer this question by assuming that we are realists with respect to *B*. Dummett (1978:360) has argued that reduction is often viewed as anti-realistic since it can be the first stage in an argument against the principle of bivalence in *A*. Thus, a reduction of *A* to *B* functions as an important premise in the argument whose conclusion is that not every proposition in *A* is either true or false. For example, a phenomenalist can use a reduction of sentences about material objects to sentences about sense data in order to reject bivalence with respect to material objects. To do so, he will assume that the following is possible: sentence *a* about material objects is translated into sentence b_1 about sense data, and sentence ~ *a* is translated into sentence b_2, which is not the negation of b_1, thus $b_1 v b_2$ can be false although *B* is bivalent.[17]

But even in cases in which this argument is valid and *A* is not bivalent, we cannot infer anti-realism with respect to *A*. This is because bivalence is not a necessary condition for realism. To convince ourselves of this, let us assume that *A* is the set of propositions that attribute baldness to people. Although there is no bivalence in *A*, we are nonetheless realistic with respect to it. A proposition on baldness, if it is true, is determined as such independently of our ability to know it.

If this is the case, the argument from reduction to anti-realism fails. I will now offer an argument that draws the opposite conclusion. I will prove that in those cases in which we are realistic with respect to *B* and *A* is reduced to *B* we must be realistic with respect to *A*.

Realism with respect to *B* means that every *B* proposition is determined as true independently of us. That is, propositions in *B* can be true without our being able to know it.

Let us focus on proposition *a* in *A* which is translated into proposition *b* in *B*. If *b* lies outside of our knowledge, so does *a*, thus propositions in *A* could be true without our being able to know it. This is a realistic position with respect to *A*. The conclusion at this point is that anti-realism is not entailed by reduction. Further, when there is a reduction to a realistic domain, we have realism with respect to *A*.

Let us now check what can be inferred with respect to *A* when *A* is reducible to *B* and we are anti-realists with respect to *B*. I will prove that in such a case we are also anti-realists with respect to *A:*

a is true
↑↓ (because of the reduction)
b is true
↑↓ (because of anti-realism with respect to *B*)
b belongs to the ideal theory
↑↓
a belongs to the ideal theory.

The final stage is justified since the reduction itself can in principle be known (see section 2.1). We have proven that every *a* proposition in *A* is true iff it belongs to an ideal theory. That is—anti-realism with respect to *A*.

Prima facie, the situation is quite simple. In order to determine whether we are realists with respect to *A*, we need only know whether we are realists with respect to *B*. But a problem arises precisely at this point. We may recall that *B* is the set of propositions which constitute evidence for propositions in *A*. If *B* is reducible to another set *C*, then in order to determine whether we are realists with respect to *B*, we must first determine whether we are realists with respect to *C*. There are two possibilities:

1. The process of reduction is never ending, that is, for every set of propositions there is another set to which it is reducible. In such a case the existence of a reduction of *A* to *B* will not help us to draw any conclusion on the question of realism.

2. The process of reduction stops. Without loss of generality, let us assume that it stops as early as *B*. I will show that the question of our realism with respect to such a set of propositions yields contradicting answers. In order to understand the difficulty, let us consider *B* a set of simple observational propositions such as "the hand of the clock shows 3".[18] Another example of a set of propositions such as *B* is the set of finitist propositions in mathematics, or the set of simple arithmetic propositions.

On the one hand, we have a realist intuition with respect to such propositions. We believe their truth to be independent of us. This intuition is in keeping with the fact that the principle of bivalence holds for them. On the other hand, it follows from the epistemic characterization of realism that we are anti-realists with respect to *B*. This is the case since *B* describes all possible evidence, and all evidence is, in principle, knowable; in an ideal epistemic state, all evidence is accessible to us. In Dummett's terms, *B* is made up of propositions which describe such truth conditions as we can identify; such conditions, by definition, cannot transcend our knowledge.

Even Dummett oscillates between realism with respect to *B* (1978:360) and the claim that the question of realism does not arise at all with respect to *B*:

> It is ... a condition of the dispute's arising at all that it is agreed by both sides that, for any given statement of the disputed class, there need not exist any true statement of the reductive class which we should count as evidence either for or against the truth of the given statement. (1978:156)

Hence, since for every proposition in set *B* there is evidence that renders it true (evidence described by the very proposition), the dispute does not even arise with respect to *B*.

The conclusion of this discussion is that a reduction of *A* cannot "create" anti-realism. If there exists a set toward which we are anti-realists, though not because we reduced it to another set, a reduction of *A* to this set will ground an anti-realist conclusion with respect to *A*. But if such a set does not exist, we will not succeed in grounding anti-realism by recourse to reduction.

Notes

1. Similar critiques of diagonal predicates and infinite disjunction have been raised by Teller (1983), Kincaid (1987) and Van Cleve (1990).
2. I am not even convinced of this assumption of closure. A very long disjunction is not always accessible to us and cannot be projected. But I have no general argument against closing the sets under finite disjunctions. For the purpose of my arguments that supervenience does not entail reduction the assumption that we cannot close *A* and *B* under infinite disjunction and conjunction is sufficient.
3. Note that I did not show that these generalizations can obtain without supervenience if we require more of them (that they be causal, for example).
4. This entailment is on the condition that every combination in first order language of *B*-predicates belongs to *B*.
5. Unless it is shown that these characterizations supervene on the physical predicates.

6 I have so far shown that all versions of (local) supervenience, with the exception of supervenience$_3$, hold with respect to eternal sentences. It is interesting to note what takes place when discussing the set of necessary sentences. For example, let us momentarily restrict our discussion to the set of arithmetical sentences. In such a case, supervenience$_3$ also holds. The truth of arithmetical sentences supervenes in all senses on their syntactical properties.

7 On the distinction between the narrow and broad sense of a property, see section 2.3.

8 The degree of holism may be measured by the quantity of conceptual connections between the claims in the domain, or by their density.

9 See Kripke, for example (1980:144–145).

10 This argument also applies to Moore's 'open question argument' against reduction.

11 The argument is important however, since it is relevant against certain explanations of the phenomenon of supervenience. See 3.2.

12 See Susan Haack's survey (1973).

13 For example, the pragmatist definition of truth negates metaphysical realism. See Peirce (1955:39, 288) and James (1970 [1909]).

14 There is a connection between reductionism and the characterization of realism as a position on reference (rather than truth). According to the realism of reference, expressions in language refer to genuine components of reality (do tables really exist? do electrons really exist?, etc.). An anti-realist in this sense would argue that all statements about tables, for example, are reducible to statements on sense data, and that since the domain of quantification determines ontological commitment, it follows that we are ontologically committed to sense data rather than to tables. Since I am treating realism with respect to truth rather than reference, I will not discuss the connection between reductionism and these versions of anti-realism.

15 Let us assume that all the evidence can be described by sentences. Since I am asking about the connection between realism and reductionism, rather then about realism in general, I will not discuss the question whether such a set of sentences always exists. Neither will I discuss the question whether the existence of such a set (or its absence) is relevant to the dispute on realism.

16 This choice corresponds to Dummett (1982:90).

17 A more general scheme of this argument is presented by Van Cleve (1992).

18 Someone who thinks that such propositions are reducible to propositions about sense data will consider *B* a set of propositions on sense data.

3 The Supervenience of Ethical Predicates

3.1 Introduction

Various philosophers in the field of ethics have claimed that the ethical predicates supervene on non-ethical ones. In fact, I have yet to come across a single meta-ethicist that would oppose this thesis. It has found consensus among philosophers with very different approaches to ethics, such as Moore (1922), the intuitionist, Hare (1952), the prescriptivist, Mackie (1977), the subjectivist, Blackburn (1985), the projectivist and Price (1986), the objectivist. Controversy does exist, however, regarding the question how to explain the phenomenon of supervenience, and particularly, what meta-ethicist conclusions can be drawn from it. This chapter will focus on various explanations of supervenience in ethics. A philosophical explanation is often (and perhaps always) a derivation of the phenomenon in need of explanation from other assumptions. The phenomenon of supervenience in ethics will likewise be explained thus: by recourse to arguments whose conclusions are the supervenience of the ethical predicates on non-ethical ones.

Before turning to the arguments, I shall clarify the supervenience thesis in ethics:

1. To begin with, I assume that there exists a set of ethical predicates. This very assumption raises various objections.

According to the first objection, there are no ethical predicates; there are only ethical propositions. The latter are created by the application of an ethical operator to non-ethical propositions. For example, "people murder" is not an ethical proposition. Applying the operator "forbidden" to this proposition creates the ethical proposition that murder is forbidden.

I counter this objection by claiming that I am not committed to the fact that the logical analysis of ethical propositions as containing ethical predicates is any better that other logical analyses. In order to discuss the supervenience of ethical predicates, the very possibility of an analysis of an ethical proposition as containing ethical predicates is sufficient. And such an analysis is indeed possible: for example, the proposition "murder is forbidden" can be analyzed as the application of the ethical predicate "is forbidden" or "is evil" to any event of murder. Another answer to this objection is that even if we insist that ethical propositions exist whereas ethical predicates do not, it is still possible to discuss the question of the global supervenience of ethical propositions on non-ethical ones. The discussion in the present chapter regarding the explanation of supervenience can be applied to global supervenience as well.

Another objection that arises at this point is that there is no clear distinction between an ethical and a non-ethical predicate; further, we are likely to get different definitions of this distinction from each of the various meta-ethical positions.

Though I admit that I do not know how to define ethical predicates, this does not get in the way of presenting a supervenience thesis. To do so, it is enough to assume that there is a list (possibly an open one) of predicates that we can agree are ethical, even if there is no agreement on a particular characteristic common to all of them. The question of supervenience pertains to the relation between these predicates and others.

2. Similar questions arise regarding the set of predicates on which the ethical predicates supervene. Does such a set include all the non-ethical predicates (for example, aesthetic ones)? Writers on supervenience in the moral domain have considered this set to be the set of natural predicates.[1] It is difficult, however, to determine what it is that characterizes the natural predicates as a set. The accepted definition characterizes a natural predicate as one which can be discovered empirically if it applies to an object. Natural predicates are more strictly defined as predicates whose application can be determined by the methods of the natural sciences. As in the discussion of the characteristics of ethical predicates, I need not commit myself to any particular definition: for my purposes, the existence of an extensive list of predicates which are commonly considered natural predicates is sufficient.

3. In order to clarify the thesis of supervenience, another assumption of an altogether different sort is required: the assumption that truth or falsehood can be attributed to ethical propositions. That is, contrary to Ayer for example, that ethical propositions are not pseudo-propositions (1936:143). This assumption is necessary to express the thesis of supervenience. We would like to say that two objects which are indiscernible with respect to their natural descriptions are also ethically indiscernible. But in order to do so, we must be able to say that ethical predicates apply to them. Philosophers such as Ayer and Carnap have objected to this.

To clarify my own position, I will anchor the aforementioned assumption in the meta-ethical dispute between descriptivists and anti-descriptivists. Like Mackie (1977:23–24), I take this dispute to be about the meaning of ethical propositions. More specifically, it debates the question which speech acts are created when an ethical proposition is claimed. A descriptivist would argue that such a speech-act is nothing more than the description of an object, whereas the anti-descriptivist says that when we make an ethical claim, we are doing something more: we are ordering (imperative), recommending, expressing emotion, threatening and the like. A descriptivist is committed to the fact that ethical propositions, like all descriptive propositions, have truth value.[2] Thus the descriptivist can discuss the question of supervenience (although he may not answer it in the affirmative). With respect to the anti-descriptivist, the situation is more complex. If he dispenses with the entire concept of truth or rightness in ethics, he is unable to speak of supervenience. Every anti-descriptivist, however, who believes that ethical propositions have truth value despite their not being descriptive, can pose the question of supervenience.

To conclude, the third assumption, without which supervenience cannot be discussed, is the meta-ethical assumption which refutes the position of the radical anti-descriptivist. An acceptance of this assumption, however, does not obligate me to choose between descriptivism or some less extreme form of anti-descriptivism. Neither does it require me to answer other questions regarding the concept of truth in ethics, such as: is truth in ethics absolute or relative? If relative, then relative to what—the speaker, society, the epoch? Is the concept of truth in ethics realistic?

Supervenience$_1$ of ethical predicates on natural predicates is the thesis that if two actions (or two people) are indiscernible with respect to their natural predicates, the same ethical predicates apply to them as well. We do not only pronounce moral judgments on actions that have taken place, however, we also judge those that will take place, and those that will not. When facing an ethical dilemma, we not only evaluate the action we are going to take, but also the one we have decided against taking. Furthermore, our moral judgments with respect to people do not only apply to actual people, but also to possible ones. We make judgments on people in counterfactual situations. Hare (1952:145), for example, claims that not only do we judge St. Francis as a good man, we also believe that if x (who is an immoral person in our world) had the same natural properties as St. Francis, he would also be a good man. It follows that our moral judgments apply not only to x in our world, but also to x in the possible world in which he behaves like St. Francis.

If all of our moral judgments, and not merely those referring to actual objects/actions, are subject to supervenience, we must accept stricter versions of supervenience. Let us now turn to several attempts to explain the source of a supervenience thesis that is at least as strong as supervenience$_2$.

3.2 Hare

Hare argues that the phenomenon of supervenience in ethics is not the least bit mysterious, since:

> It is simply, under another name, one of the main constituents of our old friend universalizability. (Hare, 1984:3)

In this section I will explain universalizability, examine Hare's arguments for the universalizability of ethical terms, and study the extent to which supervenience is a constituent of the requirement of universalizability.

3.2.1 *The Requirement of Universalizability*

Universalizability of predicate *R* requires the following:

If *x* is *R*, then if *y* is similar to *x* in all the relevant respects, *y* is *R*.

This is the definition put forth by Hare in *Freedom and Reason* (1963:11). In *Moral Thinking,* he dispenses with the stipulation that *y* be similar to *x* in all the relevant respects, defining the requirement as such:

If *x* is *R*, then *y* that is similar to *x* in all respects described by universal predicates is *R* (1981:21).[3]

3.2.2 *Hare's Arguments for the Universalizability of Ethical Predicates*

Hare (1963:24) argues that the ethical propositions/predicates can be universalized by virtue of their descriptive component. As I mentioned in the beginning of the chapter, the property of descriptivity applies primarily to propositions, and only by extension to properties. A property is descriptive if it is used in a speech act of description, rather than any other kind, such as a threat, a recommendation, advice, etc. According to Hare, ethical propositions are not descriptive but do have a secondary descriptive component. By stretching the use of descriptivity, Hare discusses ethical predicates, arguing that ethical predicates are not descriptive. This "stretching" can be understood thus: an ethical predicate is not descriptive since a proposition that claims "the ethical predicate *M* applies to object/action *x*" is not describing but recommending.

According to Hare, ethical propositions recommend, yet they do have a secondary descriptive component. Therefore, Hare's first argument for the universalizability of ethical predicates is the following:

1. Every descriptive predicate can be universalized.
2. Ethical predicates have a descriptive component.

Thus ethical predicates can be universalized.

The argument is not valid. Had the second assumption been "ethical propositions are descriptive", we would have a valid syllogism. But the assumption merely states that ethical propositions have a descriptive component. This fact alone entails nothing regarding the question whether they can be universalized, and does not provide any explanation as to their supervenience on other propositions.

But Hare also provides another angle of explanation on the universalizability of ethical predicates. Rather than viewing the description as the source of the supervenience of ethical predicates, he sees it in the important function of arguments and reasoning in ethical discourse. His main argument is that the thesis of universalizability is entailed by the meaning of moral words. One of the logical properties of the word "ought" for example, is that:

> it is a misuse of the word 'ought' to say "You ought, but I can conceive of another situation, identical in all its properties to this one, except that the corresponding person ought not". (Hare, 1981:10)

Hare admits, however, that it is problematic to determine the logical properties of a word. He claims that we do so, however, with the help of logical-linguistic intuitions. It is fundamental to Hare's approach that the intuitions made use of in this context be exclusively linguistic, rather than moral. In order to know whether moral words comply with the requirement of universalizability, we must understand the language we are speaking; we need not be moral ourselves.

Hare offers an additional argument for the claim that moral words are subject to the requirement of universalizability based on the assumption that such words imply generalization. He claims that moral words are in this respect similar to words that express other types of necessity. Logical necessity and causal necessity also assume generalization, or at least the existence of a generalization.

> there cannot be any necessity about his being there unless there is some law-like, universal proposition which holds, such that his not being there would be, in this situation, a breach of it. If there is no law-like proposition which holds, there is no necessity, though he might be there all the same. (Hare, 1981:8)

To my mind, the assumption that moral words imply generalizations is supported by an important argument. This argument appears in various places in Hare's writings. For example:

> ... moral judgments about particular things are made for reasons, and the notion of a reason, as always, brings with it the notion of a rule which lays down that something is a reason for something else. (Hare, 1963:21)

Elsewhere, the legitimacy of the requirement for reasons is described as part of the meaning of moral words (as opposed to imperatives):

> Plain imperatives do not have to have reasons or grounds ... but 'ought' judgments, strictly speaking, would be being misused if the demand for reasons or grounds were thought of as out of place. (Hare, 1963:36–7)

The argument that the requirement of universalizability applies to ethical predicates is the following: the application of ethical predicates always requires justification. The justification of *A* always involves a reference to something *else—B*, and to the rule which connects the two. Therefore the ethical predicate *A* cannot be applied without assuming that there exists a rule which justifies this application. If there exists a rule that justifies the application of *A* to *x*, it will also justify the application of *A* to *y*, given that *x* and *y* are identical with respect to all the universal predicates that apply to them.

To the extent that this argument is valid, it grounds a more informative requirement of universalizability than the one defined by Hare. According to the latter, predicate *R* can be universalized if when *x* is *R*, and *x* and *y* are identical with respect to universal properties, *y* is also *R*. The former argument, however, grounds the following requirement: if *x* is *R* and *y* is identical to *x* with respect to all the universal properties *that differ from R*, then *y* is *R*. The difference is significant since the first requirement presents a property of *R*, whereas the second presents a relation between *R* and other predicates. The second requirement is therefore more relevant to supervenience, which is also a relation between predicates rather than a property of predicates.

Hare oscillates between the two versions of the requirement. When discussing the descriptive component of ethical predicates, he prefers the first version (for example 1963:23), whereas in discussing the rational component of ethical propositions, which is subject to reasons, he prefers the second (1984:1). To convince ourselves that the two versions are indeed different, we need only note that "red", for example, is a descriptive predicate, although its application does not require justification. It therefore complies with the requirement of universalizability in its first version, but not in its second. Since Hare's primary contribution to meta-ethics has been the presentation of a model which enables rational discourse on moral issues, I have no doubt that the second version is the more important one. The rules of rational discourse on such issues ensure that in most cases, the same conclusions will be arrived at. It is the second version that underscores the rational aspect of ethical discourse.

As was mentioned earlier, the second version ensures supervenience. Therefore it is suitable for my needs. Further: the most important argument for supervenience, which will be duly presented, can be extracted from this last argument. In the meantime, let us take note of the fact that the most important move in the argument involves the fact that when speaking of moral judgments, the requirement of justification is always legitimate. This is a fact about the way ethical propositions are justified, and therefore about their meaning. We shall later see that facts such as these are the most relevant to explanations of supervenience.

Before critiquing Hare's main argument for the requirement of universalizability, I will develop the argument, showing that if it is valid, then it also grounds the supervenience of ethical predicates on non-ethical ones. Hare's argument is based on the claim that in order to justify the application of an ethical predicate A to an object, we must believe that another predicate B exists which applies to the object, and that there is a rule which connects A to B. If B is an ethical predicate, then there must be another predicate C (which differs from B), which applies to the object, and there must be a rule which connects B and C. It follows from the added plausible assumption that there is no infinite or circular chain of justifications that we will ultimately arrive at a non-ethical predicate. We are thus allowed to assume that B is such a predicate. This leads us to the conclusion that every application of an ethical predicate A assumes the existence of a rule $(x)(Bx \rightarrow Ax)$, when B is not an ethical predicate.

The above entails the supervenience of ethical predicates on non-ethical ones: let us assume that x and y are identical with respect to their non-ethical properties. Let us assume further that x is A. There exists a rule which justifies the attribution of A to x. Let us assume that this rule is $(x)(Bx \rightarrow Ax)$. B is a non-ethical predicate which applies to x, and it therefore also applies to *y*. We can deduce from this rule that *y* is also *A*, and this is the claim of the supervenience of ethical predicates on non-ethical ones.[4]

3.2.3 *A Critique of Hare's Argument*

Hare offers a model for rational moral discourse. He distinguishes between the questions "how should we think of moral problems?" and "what should we think of moral problems?" The model, however, treats only the first question: how a moral question should be addressed. So far, I have presented only one aspect of this model: the claim that the justification of an ethical predicate's attribution to *x* refers to a rule which connects between this predicate and a non-ethical one. Although Hare's model is far more deep and complex, in order to present the first stage in the critique, it is sufficient to note that the model enables us to deduce supervenience from facts about justification procedures.

When supervenience is grounded on justification, the distinction between two versions of supervenience is obscured. The first is a thesis about our judgments: set *A* supervenes on set *B* iff for every *x* and every *y*, if they are indiscernible with respect to *B* and the attribution of any predicate from *A* to *x* is justified, then the attribution of the same predicate to *y* is justified to the same extent. The second version is a thesis about the objects themselves: set *A* of predicates supervenes on set *B* iff for every *x* and every *y*, if they are indiscernible with respect to *B*-predicates, they are also indiscernible with respect to *A*-predicates.

In order to understand the difference between the two versions, let us observe the following case:

B is the set of predicates describing the side on which a coin landed before *t*.

A is the set of predicates describing the side on which a coin landed after *t*.

Let us assume that coin *x* was tossed 10^{10} times before *t*, and at each time landed on heads, and that the same occurred with coin *y*. In such a case, *x* and *y* are indiscernible with respect to *B*. It is justified to claim that after *t*, *x* will also land on heads. It is also justified to claim, for the same reasons, that *y* will land on heads after *t*. But it is not true that if *x* will land on heads after *t*, so will *y*. The first version of supervenience holds, but the second, which concerns the question of how the coin will really land, does not.[5] My criticism of Hare's argument is that it proves the first version of supervenience, but not the second, which is the accepted one.

For Hare, this is not damaging criticism. As an anti-realist with respect to ethics, he can claim that in this field, there is no difference between perfect justification and truth. Hare has compared his theory to ethical theories on the ideal spectator (1963:94). Such theories identify the *true* ethical judgment in a given situation with the judgment arrived at by the ideal spectator. There are disagreements as to what should be required of the ideal spectator: it is agreed that she must know all the facts, understand ethical terminology and have an imagination; the disagreement pertains to whether she ought to be empathic or emotionally neutral. For our purposes, it is sufficient that the ideal spectator's judgment be identified with truth in order to justify the move from the first thesis to the second. It follows that in order to arrive at supervenience, an anti-realistic assumption with respect to the ethical must be added to Hare's argument. I will later provide more detailed treatment of the role of the anti-realist assumption in arguments for supervenience.

The second critique refers to Hare's assumption that every justification of the application of an ethical predicate to *x* requires the existence of a rule connecting non-ethical predicates to the ethical predicate. I do not agree that the concept of justification requires any reference to rules. We should note that even Hare argues that in order to justify a moral judgment, we need not refer to rules: it is sufficient to know that such exist. I am not convinced, however, that justification requires rules even in this weaker sense. There is no doubt that justification procedures without rules exist: the attribution of an *A*-predicate to *x* is occasionally justified by referring to other properties of *x*, but these are not considered as constituting a sufficient condition for *A*.

Dancy (1981:375–377), in his critique of the requirement of universalizability, has explained why the connection between moral justification and rules is not as close as Hare assumes. Dancy presents the following example: *x* attributes the property "good" to a particular young woman due to her being chaste and pious. Her modesty and loyalty constitute reasons for attributing the ethical predicate. But there is no reason to therefore deduce that it would be justified to attribute this predicate to every chaste and pious young woman; we may well come across a young woman who is chaste and pious, but cruel. We would not attribute the same ethical predicate to her as we did to the former woman. Note that this move does not contradict the fact that in the case of the first young woman, chastity and piety did constitute justification for the judgment that she is good.

In my critique of Hare's argument, I am in agreement with Dancy that:

> … it is not the case that where my reasons for calling an action good are that it has properties *ABC* I am committed to calling any other action which has the properties *ABC* good. (Dancy, 1981:377)

My third criticism involves the argument's assumption that there exists an exhaustive lawlikeness between ethical and non-ethical predicates. That is, that in every case in which an ethical predicate applies to x, the predicate has a sufficient condition formulated in non-ethical terms. It seems to me that Hare would not want to accept so tight-knit a relation between ethical and other predicates. Although this relation is weaker than a reduction, arguments against reduction can apply to it as well.[6]

In light of these critiques, I will now attempt to present an argument similar to that of Hare in that it will refer to justification procedures in order to deduce supervenience. Unlike Hare however, these justification procedures will not assume rules, and will therefore allow me to prove the existence of a more reasonable relation between ethical and non-ethical predicates. I will prove that ethical predicates supervene on non-ethical ones despite the absence of exhaustive regularity.

3.3 Critique of Blackburn and Dancy

In this section I will present a critique of two additional arguments for the supervenience of ethical predicates on non-ethical ones. The first is Dancy's argument from resultance to supervenience (1981), and the second is Blackburn's argument from projectivism to supervenience (1984). We shall see that both arguments are valid only if they are understood as referring to our justification procedures, and as such they are not valid without the anti-realist assumption.

3.3.1 *Dancy: An Argument from Resultance to Supervenience*

Dancy has proposed an argument for supervenience based on a different property of ethical predicates. He calls this property "resultance", and defines it thus:

> The F-ness of an object results from properties $P_1 ... P_n$ of that object iff the object is F in virtue of its possession of $P_1 ... P_n$, where F-ness is not identical with $P_1 ... P_n$ nor with any truth function of members of $P_1 ... P_n$. (Dancy, 1981:367)

Every ethical property applies to an object in virtue of the application of non-ethical properties to that object. Dancy does not explain the relationship "in virtue of"; he merely emphasizes that the relation is not an epistemic one, and particularly, that it has no connection to the relation of justification:

> Nor can we in general say, where an action has a moral property *M* in virtue of having non-moral properties, *A*, *B* and *C* that the presence of *A*, *B* and *C* count generally as reasons for calling actions *M*. (Dancy, 1981:376)

According to Dancy, the significance of this relation is that as opposed to supervenience, it applies to each case separately. That is, the fact that the non-moral properties *A*, *B* and *C* make an object *M* is the specific property of that particular object (under certain conditions). The property is being *M* in virtue of the properties *A*, *B* and *C*. But there is no guarantee that another object to which *A*, *B* and *C* apply will also be *M* in virtue of *A*, *B* and *C*.

Dancy has derived the supervenience of ethical predicates on non-ethical ones from the fact that ethical properties apply to an object in virtue of non-ethical ones:

> (We) know that the relationship between a moral property and those from which it is parti-resultant is necessarily repeated in another object which resembles the first in all non-moral respects. Not only must the second object have the same moral property; it must have it for the same reasons, since there is ex hypothesis no question of a defeater. (Dancy, 1981:382)

This argument has several weaknesses:

1. The importance of the resultance relation lies in its specificity; in the fact that even when it exists in a certain object, it need not exist in another. If that is the case, why is this relation "necessarily repeated in another object"?

2. Dancy would probably give the following response: It is true that *x* being *M* in virtue of its being *A*, *B* and *C* does not entail that every *y* that is *A*, *B* and *C* is also *M*. But *y* that is *A*, *B* and *C*, and does not differ from *x* in any other respect, is also *M*. The only justification to this response is that if *y* is *A*, *B* and *C*, and does not differ from *x* in any of its other properties, then there is no property whose attribution to *y* would prevent the attribution of *M* to *y*. This is certainly the case. But to deduce that *y* is *M* from the fact that there is no justification not to attribute *M* to *y* requires, as we recall, an anti-realist assumption. And if this is Dancy's argument, he has not succeeded in proving supervenience without referring to our justification procedures.

3. To my mind, Dancy proves supervenience by recourse to a relationship that is even vaguer than supervenience. The relation "*p* is true in virtue of

q" is neither a causal relation nor a generalization. The best way to clarify it, to my mind, is by using supervenience, and therefore I do not see the point of using it to prove supervenience.

4. As we may recall, we are searching for arguments for supervenience in order to demystify this relation; in order to understand its source. Dancy's claim is that the source of supervenience lies in another relation, whose source is also unclear. Dancy has gone so far as to admit:

> It looks as if we shall have to make a bald claim to a priori knowledge of moral resultance (1981:385)

Let me emphasize that I agree with Dancy's claim that the supervenience of the moral on the non-moral is an *a priori* thesis. But I take issue with his claim that its source cannot be explained, and therefore our belief in it cannot be justified.

3.3.2 *Blackburn: An Argument for Supervenience from Projectivism*

Blackburn has presented a projectivist position in ethics (1984), claiming that such a position explains the supervenience of ethical predicates better than competing ones. Before discussing the comparison between the projectivist explanation of supervenience and others, let us first look at Blackburn's explanation.

Projectivism is a type of anti-descriptivism in ethics. According to the descriptivist, ethical judgments attribute ethical properties to objects (or actions). The anti-descriptivist, by contrast, views ethical judgments less as descriptions and more as expressions of a certain approach or attitude of the speaker. According to the projectivist, ethical judgments are the projection of the speaker's interests on the objects.

Blackburn, however, is not a subjectivist: he does not claim that there is no sense in speaking of the truth of ethical judgments, nor that the very fact of sincerely projecting one's feelings on an object turns that projection into a correct one. He offers, rather, a concept of truth similar to that in the theory of the ideal judge:

> a best possible set of attitudes, thought of as the limiting set which would result from taking all possible opportunities for improvement of attitude. (Blackburn, 1984:198)

This is an anti-realist definition of truth, since it identifies truth with ideal justification rather than the existence of a state of affairs in the world to which the claim corresponds. As I will show in the following section, supervenience can be deduced from anti-realism with respect to ethics combined with facts on the justification of ethical propositions. Blackburn, however, proposes another sort of argument. According to it, the very role of ethical judgments entails their supervenience on other judgments. He argues that the requirement for supervenience is a constraint on our ethical judgments, and that if these judgments do not comply with the constraint of supervenience:

> it would betray the whole purpose for which we moralize, which is to choose, commend, rank, approve, forbid things on the basis of their natural properties. (Blackburn, 1985:56)

Elsewhere, he writes that anyone who would judge x as good but would judge y that is identical to x in all its natural properties as not good is "convicted of misidentifying a caprice as a moral opinion" (1971:115). The function of the projectivist assumption in these passages, which aim to explain supervenience, is unclear. Here are a few possibilities:

1. It follows from projectivism that when *a* judges that x is good, he does so because of x's natural properties. Thus if y is identical to x in its natural properties, what caused *a* to have a positive attitude toward x will prompt him to have the same attitude toward y.

The argument's first weakness is that there is no guarantee that if an A-type event is the cause of a B-type event, every time an A-type event appears, a B-type event will also appear. That is, the fact that *a* regarded x in a particular light because of its property N, for example, does not ensure that *a* will regard y, which also has property N, in the same light. It may be that *a* viewed x positively because of *a*'s properties at that moment and not only because of x's properties.

The argument's second weakness is that even when *a* regards y positively, that is, when *a* judges that y is good, we cannot deduce that y is indeed good. As I mentioned earlier, Blackburn is not a subjectivist, and he maintains the gap between "*a* thinks that y is good" and "y is good".

2. By regarding the "because" in the projectivist assumption as belonging to justification rather than cause, the argument can be constructed differently: The projectivist assumption ensures that when *a* judges x to be good, he does so in virtue of x's natural properties. That is, x's natural properties justify *a*'s judgment on x's moral value. Thus if y is identical to x in its natural properties, then the same properties in x that justified the judgment

that *x* is good will also justify the judgment that *y* is good. As I will show in the following section, this argument becomes valid only with the addition of an anti-realist assumption.

To conclude, this section has shown us that there is no argument for supervenience from projectivism or from resultance that is not based on our justification procedures. I will now construct an argument for supervenience that is based on our justification procedures.

3.4 An Argument for Supervenience from Justification

Let us return to Hare's argument (3.1), which derives supervenience from facts about the justification of ethical propositions. Despite my critique of the argument's exaggerated use of rules, its general line of argumentation is correct: under certain conditions, facts about justification entail supervenience. So far, I have only presented a small section of Hare's model for moral thinking. In order to construct my argument, it is necessary to look into this model in further detail. The best way to present it would be to describe a moral dispute (although the model is far broader, and can be applied to any moral deliberation).

Let us assume that *A* argues that in the given situation, *x* must be done, whereas *B* argues that in the same situation, *x* must be avoided. According to subjective intuition, the dispute may well culminate at this point: *A* expresses a particular feeling regarding *x*, and *B* expresses a different feeling regarding *x*. Hare, however, claims that the requirement to justify a moral judgment is always legitimate, thus, at this stage *A* must provide a justification of his judgment that *x* is the right thing to do under the given circumstances (and *B* must provide justification for the opposing judgment). Such a justification has a specific form: *A* must describe a natural aspect of *x* (N_1), and argue that action *x* is justified by the fact that it is N_1. Since every justification implies a rule, *A* is committed to the following generalization: in every situation which is identical to the present one with respect to its universal characteristics, the action with the property N_1 is the correct one.

B, who is arguing the opposite, can deploy the following tactic: he can describe a situation identical to the present one with respect to all of its universal characteristics, but different with respect to the identity of the participants (for example, a situation in which *A* himself will suffer from the results of action *x*), arguing that in such a situation *A* will not recommend the N_1 action. This is the tactic to which Hare refers when he claims that "all moral arguments are ad hominem" (1963:111).

Two options are now available to *A*: the first is to maintain his position with respect to N_1 despite the new situation described by *B*. In such a case, *B* has not succeeded in refuting *A*'s argument. The second option is to refuse to recommend the N_1 action in the new situation, but to make this refusal contingent upon the difference between the original situation and the new one. This difference creates a discrepancy between the description of action x in the original situation and that of the action similar to x in the new situation. The discrepancy can be described by a new predicate N_2, such that action x in the original situation is N_1 & N_2, whereas the relevant action in the new situation is N_1 & N_2. *A* can claim that the rule justifying action x in the original situation is not "every action which is N_1 is correct in a situation similar to the given one", but "every action which is N_1 & N_2 is correct in a situation similar to the given one".

This brings us back to the starting point of the argument: *B* will attempt to refute the new rule. It is important to note that the rule is *not* refuted when *B* describes a situation completely different from the given one, in which the application of the rule leads to an undesired result. The rule is legitimately refuted when the situation presented is "identical" to the original one but *A* will no longer follow the rule. This is so since in such an argument, we are not looking for the correct moral theory or a system of rules which can apply to any situation; rather, we are attempting to justify a particular action in the given situation. Thus a suitable rule is one which will recommend such an action in any situation that is *similar* to the given one.[7]

Such a move is familiar to us from a host of ethical arguments, thus there is no need to present examples (for a detailed example, see Hare, 1963:90–111). For my purposes, the formal structure of the argument is important. Not only is this type of argument familiar, it also seems legitimate and rational. By drawing a comparison to philosophy of science, we can clarify Hare's aim. Hare's claim (1963:87), which is to some degree justified, is that moral discourse is similar to scientific discourse as presented by Popper: the scientist (or ethicist) puts forth a hypothesis (rule). Such a move is not justified: the hypothesis (rule) is merely a guess. Scientific (or ethical) discourse consists of an attempt to refute the hypothesis (rule).

There are, clearly, important differences, and Hare is aware of these. My interest, however, is to stretch the analogy so that it applies to the philosophers of science and ethics. The philosopher of science searches for the structure of rational scientific discourse, and he does so by a critical study of the scientist's operations. He assumes that the scientist's concrete operations are relevant to his abstract model, although the model will not be impaired even if many scientists diverge from it. In the same way, the philosopher of ethics searches for a model of rational ethical discourse. Such a model is not refuted if many people diverge from it, unless these people are rational. Thus the model offered by the ethicist, like the one offered by the philosopher of science, must correspond to our rational judgments. It must correspond to our judgments on the degree of rationality of a particular moral (or scientific) discourse.

I agree with Hare's fundamental position that the supervenience of ethical on non-ethical predicates can be derived from the model of moral reasoning. As we saw in the previous section, this depends on an anti-realist assumption with respect to the ethical domain. In Chapter Five, I will show that this dependence can provide the grounds for an anti-realist approach to the ethical domain. At present I will only construct the argument. The difference between my argument for supervenience and Hare's follows from my use of a different model of moral reasoning. This difference will also influence the type of supervenience I will ground.

I propose the following model for the justification of ethical propositions: Let us assume once again that *A* argues that *x* must be done in a particular situation, while *B* argues that the same situation calls for an avoidance of action *x*. I agree with Hare that the requirement for justification is always legitimate, and that *A* justifies his judgment by claiming that *x* is N_1, where N_1 is a non-ethical predicate. Unlike Hare, I am not claiming that by doing so, *A* is committed to a rule of any kind. *B* will use a variety of ways to draw *A*'s attention to other situations in which an N_1 action is not recommended from an ethical standpoint. *A* can show *B* that in all these other situations the N_1 action is not N_2, whereas in the given situation *x* is N_2, and that in fact, the claim that *x* is a moral action is justified by the fact that *x* is N_1 and N_2, etc.

Here is an example of such an argument: *A* argues that *B* must give him 1,000 dollars. *A*'s justification is that last week, he lent *B* 1,000 dollars (that is, N_1 = one week ago 1,000 dollars were lent to *B* by *A*). *B* gives *A* examples of situations in which it is not obligatory to return loans: for example, a situation in which the lender plans to use the money to harm someone ($\sim N_2$). *A* shows *B* that the given situation is unlike this, but rather, it is $N_1 \& N_2$, and that which justifies *A*'s demand is ($N_1 \& N_2$). Neither *A* nor *B* refer to generalizations at any point in the argument. Although they may refer to *prima facie* generalizations (Ross, 1930:Chap. 2), they do not refer to true generalizations without exceptions.

To my mind, the model I have proposed for the justification of ethical propositions, also describes the justification of aesthetic propositions by recourse to non-aesthetic ones,[8] and that of counterfactual statements by recourse to categorical propositions.

Let us assume that *A* claims that if I had come to the party, I would have enjoyed myself, whereas I argue that he is wrong. In order to justify his claim, *A* refers to a categorical proposition: there was good music at the party. I refer to another categorical proposition: I had a headache. The claim that the music was good does not justify the counterfactual statement: in order to do so we require the proposition that there was good music and I didn't have a headache. At this point, *A* can either agree that I would not have enjoyed myself, or refer to another categorical proposition. The model is identical: in order to justify propositions of a certain kind, we refer to propositions of another kind. We need neither refer to generalizations, nor assume that they exist.[9]

The similarity between my model and that of Hare lies in the fact that it is always legitimate to require a justification of a moral judgment, and in the fact that this requirement is always met, ultimately, by recourse to non-ethical propositions. My model differs, however, in that it does not assume generalizations. That is, I do not assume that in order for rational discourse on moral issues to take place, strong generalizations, that have no exceptions about which actions are moral, must obtain.

I feel that Hare made some advances in this direction by presenting the distinction between the intuitive and the critical levels of moral reasoning. On the intuitive level, we operate in accordance with simple rules, without considering their justification or their applicability in the specific case. Such rules are necessary to us both for psychological and for practical reasons: not every situation that calls for a decision affords time for thinking. In most cases, we don't have enough time and we are neither calm nor objective enough. Further, it may be easier to teach children to act in accordance with general principles rather than to consider each separate case. The rules discussed here are simple and general (that is, their domain of application is quite broad), and most importantly—they are always false, that is, there are exceptions to the rules. (The latter characteristic explains the fact that in certain situations, such intuitive rules can conflict with one another.) Such rules are of great value, despite the existence of exceptions, since someone operating according to them has greater chances of arriving at the right decision from a moral standpoint than someone who does not.

Hare has compared such rules to strategic rules in chess (1981:38, 52): someone who plays according to good strategic rules has a better chance of winning the game than someone who does not, but winning is not defined by these strategic rules, but by the rules of the game.

> Similarly in morals, the principles which we have to follow if we are to give ourselves the best chance of acting rightly are not definitive of "the right

> act"; but if we wish to act rightly we shall do well, all the same, to follow them. (Hare, 1981:38)

In chess, winning is defined by the rules of the game; what is it that defines moral action? What in ethics is analogous to the rules of the game in chess? To my mind, it is at this point that the analogy breaks down. Hare, however, attempts to stretch the analogy, arguing for the existence of additional ethical rules: we arrive at these when thinking on the critical level. Hare calls these rules "critical principles" (1981:41), and claims that they are extremely specific, that is, their domain of application is restricted, and, as opposed to intuitive principles which are general and simple, they are very complex.[10] Although there is critical reasoning in my own justification model, there are no critical principles. The aim of critical reasoning is not to arrive at the set of correct ethical rules, but to find the right action in any given situation. Critical reasoning amounts to "knowledge how", rather than "knowledge that".

My claim corresponds to Hare's approach more easily than does his own claim for the existence of critical rules (principles). On the one hand, the claim that on the critical level only logical and linguistic intuitions, rather than ethical ones, are used, is important to Hare (1981:40). On the other hand, he emphasizes that substantive ethical conclusions cannot be derived from linguistic intuitions alone; factual propositions are required for such a derivation (1981:16). It is thus unlikely that ethical rules can be arrived at via critical reasoning; such reasoning only allows us to compare different ethical judgments. Such a conclusion corresponds to my approach, in which critical reasoning is a matter of "knowing how" (it contains inference rules, not axioms).

We will now see that supervenience can also be derived from the model I have constructed, a model which does not assume the existence of ethical rules. The following is a general presentation of the argument in order to show its strengths and weaknesses.

Let us assume that there are two domains of predicates, *A* (in this case, the domain of ethical predicates) and *B* (the domain of natural predicates). When justifying an *A*-proposition, we must ultimately refer to a *B*-proposition.[11] I will prove that domain *A* supervenes on domain *B*. I will first prove global supervenience, and will subsequently modify the assumptions so that they will entail local supervenience.

Let us assume that w_1 and w_2 are possible worlds, indiscernible with respect to the *B*-propositions. We will assume that proposition *a* from *A* is true in w_1. We will now resort to an anti-realist assumption with respect to *A*: if *a* from *A* is true, then this can, in principle, be justified. As we recall, the justification can be made by recourse to a reference to *B*-propositions.

Let us assume that $b_1 ... b_n$[12] from B justifies the judgment that a is true in w_1. w_1 and w_2 are indiscernible with respect to the B-propositions (a premise). Thus $b_1 ... b_n$ are also true in w_2, and the claim that a is true in w_2 is therefore justified and hence true (another usage of the anti-realist assumption).

Before I continue, I will present an objection to this argument. A critic would say that $b_1 ... b_n$ justify a in w_1, but not in the possible world w_2. This is the case since there are different connections between A-propositions and B-propositions in w_2, and A-propositions are justified by recourse to other B-propositions, and possibly even by propositions that are not in domain B.

The answer to this critic is that when we say that the claim "a is true in w_2" is justified, we do not mean that people in w_2 justify a. My assumption is that a is justified by recourse to B-propositions since that is the meaning of a. This is how we use A-propositions. When we justify A in w_2, we continue to use the language just as we do now; we do not begin to speak the language of w_2. Kripke has clarified this distinction in a different context:

> To clear up one thing which people have asked me: When I say that a designator is rigid, and designates the same thing in all possible worlds, I mean that, as used in *our* language, it stands for that thing, when *we* talk about counterfactual situations. I don't mean, of course, that there mightn't be counterfactual situations in which in the other possible worlds people actually spoke a different language. One doesn't say that 'two plus two equals four' is contingent because people might have spoken a language in which 'two plus two equals four' meant that seven is even. Similarly, when we speak of a counterfactual situation, we speak of it in English, even if it is part of the description of that counterfactual situation that we were all speaking German in that counterfactual situation. We say, 'suppose we had all been speaking German' or 'suppose we had been using English in a nonstandard way'. Then we are describing a possible world or counterfactual situation in which people, including ourselves, did speak in a certain way different from the way we speak. But still, in describing that world, we use English with our meanings and our references. (Kripke, 1980:77)

The proof of local supervenience is quite similar to that of global supervenience. The assumption with regard to justification will be modified as follows: propositions that attribute an A-property to x are justified by recourse to propositions which attribute a B-property to x. This assumption allows us to prove the supervenience of A on B. I will prove supervenience$_3$, which entails supervenience$_1$ and supervenience$_2$:

Let us assume that x and y are indiscernible with respect to the B-predicates, and let us assume that x is A_i in w_1. I will once again use the anti-realist assumption: if x is A_i then this proposition can, in principle, be justified. It will be justified by the attribution of B-predicates to x. Since the same B-predicates can be attributed to y, the attribution of the property A_i to y is justified. By using the anti-realist assumption again, we conclude that y is A_i.

If this is the case, then I have proved that the strongest version of supervenience can be derived from facts about justification. This derivation is enabled by the anti-realist assumption that truth in ethics is equivalent to ideal justification.

By way of concluding this section, I will emphasize an important distinction between the proof based on my model and that based on Hare's. As we recall, the concept of supervenience is midway between reduction and independence. It is important in such cases in which dependence without reduction obtains. As we saw in section 2.3, exhaustive lawlikeness (like reduction) entails supervenience, but supervenience entails neither reduction nor exhaustive lawlikeness; therefore the concept of supervenience without reduction or exhaustive lawlikeness exists. The proof based on Hare's model, however, entails supervenience with exhaustive lawlikeness. As a result, Hare does succeed in explaining the following puzzle: how can the set of predicates B determine the set of predicates A without the existence of specific connections between A-predicates and B-predicates? My own proof does provide an explanation of the unique phenomenon of supervenience: a particular model of justification creates supervenience without creating specific connections between predicates.

In this chapter, I have shown that the supervenience of ethical predicates can be derived from justification procedures only by recourse to an anti-realist assumption. I will later put forth the argument that this is indeed the best way of explaining supervenience in this domain, and that the supervenience of ethical predicates therefore supports anti-realism.

Notes

1 Hare regards the set of descriptive predicates as the base set. The term creates confusion, however, since the distinction between the descriptive and the non-descriptive exists between propositions, not predicates. See discussion in section 3.2.2.

2 As I will show later on, a descriptivist is not committed to the fact that the truth of an ethical proposition is objective and independent of us. These are questions which he can afford to leave open.

3 A universal description is one which does not refer to specific objects. Hare does not justify his use of the controversial distinction (Goodman,1983) between universal and non-universal descriptions. In order to understand Hare's meaning, I am using the

distinction intuitively, but I will not need it in order to formulate the supervenience thesis I aim to justify.

4 The status of this rule determines the version of supervenience. If it applies in our world, $supervenience_1$ holds. If it applies to all the hypothetical objects—as Hare believes—then $supervenience_3$ holds, and therefore so do $supervenience_1$, $supervenience_2$, and $supervenience_4$ which are entailed by it.

5 This distinction was presented, for other purposes, by Klagge (1988). He calls the first version ascriptive supervenience, and the second, ontological supervenience.

6 Exhaustive lawlikeness entails the supervenience of *A* on *B* even in the absence of assumptions about rational discourse. See Section 2.3.

7 Why should we contend ourselves with such rules, rather than looking for more general ones, which would apply to a broader set of situations? Hare responds to this by distinguishing between intuitive and critical thought (1981:26–43). At this stage I will assume that this is indeed the correct description of moral arguments.

8 For example: When we apply aesthetic terms, we explain why by referring to features which do not depend for their recognition upon an exercise of taste ... 'delicate because of its pastel shades and curving lines' or 'it lacks balance because one group of figures is so far off to the left and is so brightly illuminated' ... when no explanation of this kind is offered, it is legitimate to ask or search for one. (Sibley 1959:424)

9 This is precisely Levi's claim with respect to statistical inferences (1969:304). These are justified by virtue of their being an *application* of inference rules, rather than because one of their premises is a generalization or a statistical law.

10 Elsewhere, Hare claims that such a critical principle, "though universal, may be so complex that it defies formulation in words at all" (1963:39).

11 An *A*-proposition is one which is formulated by recourse to *A*-predicates. This is generally a proposition which attributes an *A*-predicate to an object.

12 I am using $b_1 ... b_n$ for the sake of simplicity. I do not think that there is always a finite set of propositions that justifies the judgment that *a* is true, irrespective of the other *B*-propositions. In a certain context, *a* can be justified by reference to $b_1 ... b_n$, whereas in another, other *B*-propositions would have to be referred to in order to justify it (for example, a context in which someone who objects to *a* will make use of other *B*-propositions that influence the judgment that *a* is true).

4 The Supervenience of Mental Predicates

4.1 A Critique of Papineau's Argument

In this chapter, I will investigate the arguments for the supervenience of the mental on the physical. Before entering into the arguments themselves, I will clarify the assumption which lies at the foundation of the entire discussion. As in the field of ethics, the distinction between mental and physical predicates in philosophy of mind is not well defined. For the purpose of this discussion, the existing consensus on the status of specific predicates—their being either physical or mental—is sufficient. As long as there are two domains of predicates, the question of their relation to each other is significant, and the supervenience thesis is a possible answer to this question. If, for example, the physics of the future or the ideal physics will include mental predicates in a way that will not allow for any distinction between these and physical predicates, the question of their relation to one another is likely to disappear, since we will be left with only one domain. As long as this is not the case (and to my mind, there is no reason to believe that it will be), supervenience is a significant and reasonable thesis, and this chapter will focus on attempts to explain its source.

The supervenience thesis, according to all the arguments I have come across, finds its source in the completeness of physics. The main assumption in these arguments is that in a certain respect (which these arguments attempt to clarify), the physical domain is complete, whereas the mental is not:

> Too much happens to affect the mental that is not itself a systematic part of the mental. (Davidson, 1982:224)

I will start by investigating a relatively simple argument proposed by Papineau (Papineau, 1990). The argument's first premise, which he formulates as follows, is that of the completeness of physics:

> All physical events are determined (or have their chances determined) entirely by prior physical events according to physical laws. (Papineau, 1990:67)

The words in parentheses give rise to the possibility of a complete and non-deterministic theory. Papineau ignores this possibility in the argument itself, and makes use of the premise of a complete physics in the same way he would use the deterministic premise: every physical event is determined by prior physical events, according to the laws of physics. Papineau claims that this argument can be expanded to include the non-deterministic case. I will not investigate this claim here, since even in the deterministic case, the argument contains serious flaws, which I will presently illustrate.

The following is the second premise used by Papineau:

> The principle of no independent causal powers: whenever any mental event causes another event, it does so in virtue of its physical features, in the sense that in the context the effect is fixed entirely by the physical features of the mental cause. (Papineau, 1990:67)

Papineau claims that the second premise is derived from the first, and that the supervenience of the mental on the physical is derived, in the following manner, from both premises: let *a* and *b* be two physically indiscernible events. Let us assume towards contradiction that there exists a mental characteristic *M* which is true of *a* but not of *b*. It follows from the second premise that *a* and *b* have the same causal effects; this is so because the causal effects of an event are strictly determined by its physical characteristics, which are identical in both *a* and *b*. Thus the mental difference between *a* and *b* cannot be expressed:

> But a difference which cannot possibly show up in any differential effects is surely no difference at all. (Papineau, 1990:67)

In the first stage of investigating the argument, I will assume that it is valid, and that it proves the conclusion that every two events which are physically indiscernible are mentally indiscernible; that is, that the mental features of an event supervene on its physical features. This raises the question: how is the supervenience of the mental features of *events* on their physical features related to the supervenience of the mental features of *objects* on their physical features? The various versions of the discussion on local supervenience have focused on objects. Further, the original question posed in the present chapter is whether two objects can be physically indiscernible but mentally discernible; that is, whether the mental features of an object are determined by its physical features. How does the fact that the mental features of an event are determined by its physical features advance the discussion of the original question?

It is important to emphasize that this question is still pertinent even if we accept Davidson's claim that events are individuals. The reverse, in fact, is the case: viewing events as particulars forms the basis of Papineau's argument as well as other arguments that prove supervenience with regard to events but not to objects. The supervenience thesis with regard to events is formulated such that if two events are physically indiscernible, they are also mentally indiscernible. In this formulation, we quantify over events, and hence assume that events are individuals having features (mental and physical).

A position that opposes that of Davidson regards events as intentional objects; that is, as objects whose identity is dependent on the way in which they are described. Such a position sees events as more similar to propositions or facts than to objects. This position does not allow the formulation of a supervenience thesis regarding events which is analogous to that regarding objects. If it were possible to formulate such a thesis, it would look like this: if two facts are physically indiscernible, then they are also mentally indiscernible. This thesis, however, does not touch on the question of physicalism. Facts attribute features to objects, but even if these have features themselves, they are abstract, neither mental nor physical.

Thus, when I ask about the connection between the supervenience thesis regarding events and the one regarding objects, I am assuming a Davidsonian view of events. Moreover, I am assuming that in spite of the fact that events are individuals, they are not identical to objects. Davidson's ontology includes both events and objects. I need not enter into the question of how objects are to be distinguished from events in such an ontology in order to ground the modest argument that a supervenience thesis regarding events is not (at least *prima facie*) a supervenience thesis regarding objects.[1]

My main criticism of Papineau's argument, therefore, is that if it succeeds in proving anything at all, it is the supervenience thesis regarding events. Such a thesis is less clear than one regarding objects, and does not express the relation of determinacy in which we are interested.

This lack of clarity is caused by the following two factors:

1. Such a thesis is dependent on our approach toward events. Different views regarding events yield different theses of supervenience.

2. If we assume, for example, a Davidsonian view of events, only supervenience$_1$ and supervenience$_2$ will be significant. Since supervenience$_3$ quantifies over possible events, it assumes the concept of the identity of events across possible worlds. This concept is far more problematic than that of the identity of objects across possible worlds. I will explain why. As Kripke (1980:17, 38–43) showed, there are no necessary and sufficient conditions

for the identity of individuals across possible worlds. According to him, identity between object a_1 in world w_1 and object a in our world can be explained by the claim that this identity is part of our description of world w_1: we imagine a world in which a given object in our world has changed in a certain respect, for example—object a has moved. Since such a change is possible, we can imagine a world w_1 in which a has moved. It is therefore clear that a in w_1 is identical to a in our world, since that is how we described w_1.

In light of Kripke's explanation, it becomes clear that the very presentation of the problem as the question of when a_1 in w_1 is identical to a in our world is misleading. I have done so only in order to show the sense in which Kripke answers the question of the identity between a_1 in w_1 and a in our world. The answer is that a_1 in w_1 is identical to a in our world if w_1 is described as a world in which a has changed, and a_1 is the new name for a after the change. Needless to say, this name is superfluous if we accept Kripke's explanation. The conclusion from his explanation is that we can only grant significance to supervenience$_3$ if we allow that changes can apply to individuals to which this thesis can be attributed. Since events do not change,[2] it is not possible to use the concept of change to explain supervenience$_3$ regarding them. For the same reason, supervenience$_4$ is also not significant regarding events.

Aside from the lack of clarity, the supervenience thesis regarding events also raises an additional problem: it does not ensure determinacy. In order to show this, let us return to the question with which I opened my critique of Papineau: is a supervenience thesis regarding objects entailed by a supervenience thesis regarding events? I will show that the answer to this question is negative, and that a supervenience thesis regarding events therefore does not ensure the relation of determinacy in which I am interested; it allows the possibility of two physically indiscernible objects which are completely different mentally.

In order to show that a supervenience thesis regarding objects is not derived from one regarding events, I will present a model in which not event the weakest supervenience holds regarding objects, despite the fact that it does hold regarding events. Let a be an object which at time t has the physical properties $P_1 \ldots P_n$ and the mental property M. At time t_1, it has the physical properties $P_1 \ldots P_n$ and the mental property $\sim M$. Thus, between t and t_1, a underwent a mental change without undergoing a physical one—contrary to supervenience$_4$. This model, however, does not contradict the claim that there cannot be two objects which are physically indiscernible but mentally discernible, since the event of a's change from M to $\sim M$ is a mental event.

The only thing that can be derived from a supervenience thesis regarding events about a solitary mental event is that it has physical characteristics,[3] but these characteristics need not be of the type "*a* changed from P_i to $\sim P_i$", and therefore it does not follow that *a* changes physically. From this example, we can conclude that even if we succeed in proving supervenience of the mental properties of events on their physical properties, we will have achieved nothing, since such a supervenience is consistent with the existence of an object that changes mentally but not physically, and with the existence of physical duplicates that mentally, are completely different.[4]

Papineau's argument has another weakness: it begs the question. An important phase in this argument is the deduction that any two events that are physically indiscernible have the same causal effects. Papineau's assumption, however, only ensures the weaker claim; that if two events are physically indiscernible, their causal effects are physically indiscernible. In order to deduce from this that these effects are mentally indiscernible, we must assume supervenience.

I will now show why it is only the weaker claim that can be derived from Papineau's assumptions. According to assumption II, the effects of an event are determined by its physical properties. That is, its physical properties, in addition to the laws of physics, ensure its effects. If by "ensure its effects", we mean that the effects can be derived, it is clear that Papineau did not achieve his aim: mental properties cannot be *derived* from physical properties and the laws of physics. Therefore, the physical properties of an event can, at best, ensure the *physical* properties of its effects.

I have presented Papineau's argument, despite its flaws, for two reasons. The first is that the critique of this argument teaches us something important; that supervenience regarding events is not relevant to my purposes. The second is that I identify with Papineau's position, which claims that the source of the supervenience of the mental on the physical and its explanation are partially located in the completeness of physics. Papineau, however, did not succeed in finding an argument that grounds this claim. In the next section I will investigate another argument for supervenience, which is grounded in a more sophisticated definition of the completeness of physics.

4.2 A Critique of Horgan's Argument

Anyone who holds a supervenience thesis must come to terms with the following: we can imagine a world which is physically indiscernible from our own (that is, all the physical propositions which are true in it are also true in our own world) where I experience seeing the color green when I observe a red object. The possibility of such a world stands in contradiction to the determination of the mental by the physical.

One can come to terms with this by making a distinction between that which can be imagined and that which is possible.[5] If all that is required of imagination is the ability to create a particular picture in one's mind, than not everything which can be imagined is possible. I can imagine a rock which does not fall although nothing is holding it up, and I can imagine myself being in Jerusalem and in Paris simultaneously. It does not follow, of course, that these are possible situations. If, however, imagination is not just an experience but rather, is constrained by our concepts and the connections between them, then I cannot learn about possibility from the experience of imagination, because in this sense, imagination is not transparent to me: I thought I imagined water that is not H_20, or that I was born to different parents, but in fact, I imagined something else.[6]

Thus, if a philosophical argument shows that a particular world is not possible, our ability to imagine such a world does not challenge this impossibility. In light of this, Horgan attempts to prove the following supervenience thesis:

> There do not exist any two physically possible worlds which are exactly alike physico-chemically but different with the way qualia are instantiated. (Horgan, 1987:494)

This thesis claims a global supervenience of predicates which attribute qualia to beings on physical predicates.

Horgan defines a physically possible world as one which fulfills the following conditions:

(1) The basic physico-chemical properties realized in it are mentioned in the laws of our world.

(2) The concrete individuals within it can be broken up into individuals of types that either exist in our world, or are mentioned in its laws.

It thus follows that a world which is physically possible is not necessarily one in which the laws of physics hold.

I will now study the course of the argument, beginning with its assumptions.

Assumption 1—The completeness of physics

Physics (either the physics of the future or ideal physics) is complete in the following sense. First, for every slice of space-time *A* and slice of space-time area *B*, if an event in the first area is a cause of an event in the second, then there exist physical events in *A* and *B*, such that the first is a cause of the second. Second, every physical event allows for a physical description, under which it instantiates a causal physical law which is as exceptionless as possible.

It is important to note that for Horgan, the relationship between a particular causal connection and a general rule is not necessarily one of subordination, along the lines of Hume, Hempel or Davidson. Horgan is merely committed to the existence of a connection between the rule and the causal connection: the rule supplies the relevant parameters for the truth values of counterfactuals.[7] A statistical law can also serve this function, provided that its probabilities do not reflect epistemological limitations, but rather, the objective probabilities in the world. Thus, "a law which is as exceptionless as possible" can either be a deterministic law, or one which is not, but which has no hidden parameters which enable it to develop into either a deterministic law or a more specific one. A theory can therefore be complete even if it contains statistical laws.[8]

We should note that psychology is not complete, nor does it aspire to completeness. In a room in which there are no thinking or sentient beings, one physical event causes another without any psychological event causing another such event. Furthermore, pain caused by the prick of a needle is a psychological event which does not allow any physical description under which it instantiates a psychological law.

The development of physics is indeed such that an increasing number of events are caught in the web of its laws. This is the grounds of the arguments in favor of the thesis of the completeness of physics. Even if one need not accept the thesis on the basis of such reasoning, an argument based on it is important to my ends. Such an argument will show in what sense the source of the supervenience of the mental on the physical lies in the completeness of the physical domain.

Assumption 2—Qualia have causal power

I will first present a rough formulation of this assumption, and I will subsequently sharpen it by recourse to counterfactuals.

The claim in this assumption is stronger than Davidson's claim that mental events have causal effects; it is that mental events have causal effects by virtue of their mental content. One of the more serious criticisms leveled at Davidson's position focused on its implication that mental events have causal power only by virtue of their physical characteristics.[9] This leads to the claim that a mental event would have the same results even if its mental properties were completely different, since the results of an event are solely determined by its physical properties. This is an epiphenomenalist position regarding the mental. Assumption (2) refutes this position. It is a highly intuitive assumption, and this, according to Horgan, is its sole virtue:

> I find myself utterly incapable of believing that the phenomenal quality of my experience never affects my behavior, and I suspect that you do too. The qualitative content of various pleasures and pains, for instance, seems undeniably to have an effect upon our subsequent behavior in pursuit of such pleasures and in avoidance of such pains. (Horgan, 1987:504)

We will now attempt to sharpen this assumption.

Let us assume that at time *t* a certain creature *c* sees the color red, and let us assume further that as a result, *c* said "here is red" at time t_1. The criterion that Horgan suggests for the epiphenomenality of qualia is the truth of the following two counterfactuals:

1. If had seen green despite the fact that the same physical predicates[10] applied to him, he would still have said "here is red".

2. If *c* had seen red but the physical predicates that applied to him at *t* would not have applied, he would not have said "here is red".

Horgan does not commit himself to any analysis of causality, and specifically not to the fact that these counterfactuals are part of the analysis of the given causal statement. He does claim however, that the truth of these counterfactuals renders the seeing of red completely superfluous from a causal point of view, thus contradicting assumption (2).

After the foregoing clarification, I will address the argument. As we have already seen, statements (1) and (2) are not true according to assumption (2). According to assumption (1), however, they must be true. The following provides a demonstration: let us begin by investigating statement (1). Let w_1 be the closest possible world in which *c* satisfies the same physical predicates, but sees green. Does *c* say "here is red"? Since *c*'s saying red at time t_1 is a physical event, then according to assumption (1), there exists a law that is as exceptionless as possible which draws a connection between the physical description of saying red and the physical predicates which apply to *c* at *t*. Assumption (1) ensures that all the physical features that apply to *c* at time t_1 in our world also apply to it at time t_1 in w_1, particularly those features that determine what sounds come out of *c*'s mouth at time t_1.

It is important to note that even if the law connecting the events in *c*'s environment at time *t* to the event of saying "here is red" is not deterministic, the counterfactual is true. This is so because this law is as exceptionless as possible. The following example will illustrate this. Assume that the generalization below is a non-deterministic law which is as exceptionless as possible: whenever the conditions $C_1 \ldots C_n$ hold, there is a 0.7 probability that *A* will occur and a 0.3 probability that *B* will occur.

We should recall that by "a law with the fewest possible number of exceptions", we mean that there is no additional parameter *D*, which, under the given conditions, would alter the probability of *A*. To be more specific, if at t the conditions $C_1 \ldots C_n$ and *D* hold and at t_1, *A* occurs, the following counterfactual is true: if ~*D* would occur under the given conditions, *A* would occur.

The counterfactual that Horgan discusses is completely analogous to this one. Physical predicates which apply to *c* at time *t* are connected to the saying of "red" in a law as exceptionless as possible. It follows that there are no relevant parameters to this law other than the ones referred to by it. The seeing of red by *c* is an event which functions exactly as *D* does in my example, thus counterfactual (1) is true.

It is possible to show, in a similar way, that statement (2) is true. It thus follows that the qualia of seeing red was epiphenomenal, in contradiction to assumption (2).

In order to show, however, how we may bridge the gap between assumptions (1) and (2), we will return to the investigation of the truth value of statement (1). There we assumed that there exists a possible world where the antecedent of the statement is true. This is precisely the assumption we must forgo. By doing so, it follows that in every possible world with the same true physical propositions as in our own, *c* sees red, and this entails the global supervenience of the mental on the physical.

This argument does not assume the existence (or lack thereof) of psychophysical laws, and thus the supervenience that Horgan proved by recourse to it accords with the impossibility of a reduction of the mental to the physical. The argument does, however, prove a very strong dependence between the physical and the mental. This dependence is even stronger than one created by a reduction. We should recall that every supervenience thesis is formulated relative to a given set *w* of possible worlds. A reduction ensures relative supervenience to the set of all nomologically possible worlds, that is, worlds with the same laws of nature as our own. The supervenience thesis that Horgan proved, however, concerns the set of all physically possible worlds. Horgan is not committed to the existence of a physically possible world in which our world's laws of nature do not hold. He does show, however, that if such worlds do exist, the supervenience thesis which he proved holds for these as well. To my mind, this is a very important conclusion, since it emphasizes the fact that the supervenience of the mental is not grounded in the nomological relations between mental and physical predicates.[11]

Horgan's conclusion is that the mental supervenes globally on the physical. I will now investigate the possibility of using this argument to ground a local supervenience thesis. The latter can be divided into two types: one concerns constraints on the differences between objects, and the other concerns constraints on the changes of a single object. Supervenience$_1$, supervenience$_2$ and supervenience$_3$ belong to the first type, whereas supervenience$_4$ belongs to the second. As I showed in Chapter One, the logical relations between the different theses are as follows: supervenience$_3$ $\rightarrow$ supervenience$_2$ $\rightarrow$ supervenience$_1$ $\rightarrow$ supervenience$_4$.

My position is that Horgan's argument can ground supervenience$_4$, but not the others. Thus, the argument imposes constraints on change, but not on difference. The argument does not rule out a situation in which c_1 and c_2 are two physically indiscernible objects but c_1 sees red whereas c_2 sees green.

I will begin by proving that supervenience$_4$ is entailed by the supervenience thesis proved by Horgan. Let us assume towards contradiction that there can be a change in sensation without a physical change. That is, there exists a being c which at time t senses Q and at time $t+e$ does not sense Q, despite the fact that c has not changed physically. In order to show that this contradicts Horgan's supervenience thesis, I will make use of the following modal claim: the change that took place in c between t and $t+e$ could have taken place earlier, for example between $t-e$ and t.[12] That is, c could have stopped sensing Q before t. Let us observe the possible world w_1 in which this possibility is realized. c (in w_1) at time t is physically indiscernible from c in our world but it does not sense Q. The possible world w_1 contradicts Horgan's supervenience thesis.

I will now show that Horgan's supervenience thesis does not ensure a thing regarding constraints on differences between objects. To do this I will show that supervenience$_1$, the weakest of those theses that concern differences between objects, does not follow from Horgan's supervenience thesis.

Let us assume that supervenience$_1$ is false. Let c_1 and c_2 be two beings in the world who cannot be distinguished by their physical predicates, and yet c_1 senses Q_1 whereas c_2 senses Q_2. Horgan proved that in every physically possible world in which c_1 is physically indiscernible from c_1 in our world, it senses Q_1, and that in every physically possible world in which c_2 is physically indiscernible from c_2 in our world, it senses Q_2. This poses no contradiction to the assumption that supervenience$_1$ is false.

It is possible to claim that although supervenience$_1$ is not entailed by Horgan's supervenience thesis, we can construct an argument similar to his in order to prove it. I will show that such an attempt involves a number of fundamental difficulties.

I will once again assume assumption (1), regarding the completeness of physics, and assumption (2), regarding the causal power of our qualia. Let us assume that supervenience$_1$ is false, that is, that there exist c_1 and c_2 which are physically indiscernible such that c_1 senses Q_1, whereas c_2 senses Q_2. I will now attempt to construct an argument similar to that of Horgan. Let us assume that Q_1 is the seeing of red and Q_2 is the seeing of green. c_1 says "here is red" *because* he sees red. Assumption (1) ensures that the event of c_1 saying red allows for physical descriptions that are connected through a law to the physical descriptions of c_2's seeing red. Is it therefore possible to deduce that c_2 also says "here is red" following a course analogous to that of Horgan regarding c in the possible world w_1?

This deduction is blocked at two of its stages. First, the law connecting the physical predicates that apply to c_1 at t and c's saying "here is red" can be a statistical one. In such a case, the law assigns a probability of less than 1 to the outcome that c_2 will say "here is red" and it is thus possible that c_2 will not say "here is red". Second, even if we assume that the law is deterministic, and that the exact same physical predicates apply to c_2 as to c_1 at the time that it says "here is red", we cannot deduce that c_2 says "here is red". This is the most fundamental difficulty. How will we justify the move from the fact that the same physical predicates apply to c_1 and c_2 at time t to the claim that c_1 and c_2 say the same sentence? The claim "c_2 says 'here is red'" is not a physical one; it is a claim which is laden with mental theory, because the correct interpretation of c_2's utterance is dependent on other claims about its mental state.

The only way to justify this claim is to add the assumption of supervenience in the following formulation: if c_1 and c_2 are physically indiscernible then their descriptions, as saying something meaningful, converge. In a more general sense—behavioral predicates supervene on pure physical predicates.

Although I have accepted Horgan's assumption that behavior can be described physically, it does not follow that behavior supervenes on physical predicates. There is no contradiction in the claim that c_1's behavior has the same physical description as that of c_2, yet they behave differently. I am not claiming that the supervenience thesis of the behavioral on the physical is mistaken.[13] I am merely claiming that without proving it, it is impossible to prove supervenience$_1$ in a way analogous to Horgan's method.

In order to evaluate the force of Horgan's original argument, I will show that it is impervious to these two difficulties. A non-deterministic rule of the type "if *C* then *A* at a probability of 0.7" does not, clearly, ensure that every time that *C* takes place, *A* takes place. But it does ensure that in the counterfactual situation in which only a parameter which is irrelevant to the rule has changed, then if *C* occurs (and *A* occurred in the actual situation) *A* will occur in the counterfactual situation.

The answer to the second difficulty runs along similar lines. It follows from the principle that the closest possible world is one in which we do not change anything that we are not obliged to change. (This principle does not apply, of course, to a description of actual objects.) When we ask what would have happened if *c* had seen green and nothing physical would have changed, we are observing the closest possible world which is physically indiscernible from our own. As we recall, in such a world *c* makes sounds which in our world, we interpret as "here is red". Since *c* belongs to the same linguistic community as our own, to interpret him as saying something else would be:

> A completely gratuitous departure from what happens in the actual world. (Horgan, 1987:512)

According to the analysis that I proposed in the preceding paragraphs, Horgan's original argument did, in fact, prove global supervenience and supervenience$_4$,[14] but no more than that. The argument does not ensure the absence of physical duplicates that are in completely different mental states. Horgan can claim that supervenience$_1$ and supervenience$_2$ are vacuously true, since there cannot be two different objects which are physically indiscernible. As I showed in Chapter One however, supervenience$_3$ remains informative even when supervenience$_1$ and supervenience$_2$ are not. And of course, Horgan cannot prove supervenience$_3$. Since there is no contradiction in the concept of physical duplicates (this is certainly the case if we are careful not to include proper names and location in space and time among the physical predicates), the question of whether these duplicates are mentally indiscernible is fundamental to the question of the determination of the mental by the physical. Horgan's argument does not supply an answer to this question.

4.3 A Reconstruction and Critique of Davidson's Argument

Davidson (1982:209–215) argues for a token-token identity thesis, that is, one which states that every mental event is identical to a physical one.

Such a thesis does not ensure the supervenience of the mental on the physical, for a simple reason. Every object (and every event) has different descriptions. Some objects (events) have both mental and physical descriptions. The identity thesis does not ensure a connection of determinacy between the two types of descriptions: the connection between the mental and the physical predicates can, according to this thesis, be weak, like the one between the temperature of an object and its mass, or strong, like that between the temperature of an object and the average kinetic energy of its molecules. In the following section I will show that despite the fact that supervenience does not follow from the identity thesis alone, it is entailed by a particular strengthening of this thesis. This strengthening serves another purpose as well: it will point toward a possible solution to a difficulty in Davidson's original argument, offering a valid version of this argument. Thus, in order to prove a supervenience thesis from Davidson's position, I will first address a particular difficulty in his argument and offer a solution to it. This solution will justify a strong interpretation of the identity thesis with which I shall prove supervenience.

Davidson offers a new approach to the connection between the mental and the physical. This approach arises from a reconciliation between the following three theses:

1. Psychophysical causality exists.

2. There are no psychophysical or psychological laws; thus all the laws of nature are formulated in physical terms.[15]

3. Causality is subordination under a law.

Davidson refines the third thesis using the following clarification: event *a* is a cause of event *b* if and only if there is a description *P* of *a* and a description *Q* of *b* such that every time an event of type *P* takes place, an event of type *Q* takes place, and this generalization is not a strict law. Causality is an extensional relation between two events, since the answer to the question whether an event has a particular description is independent of the way it is described. However, the existence of a law connecting the given descriptions of two events (alongside the existence of an explanation and a prediction), is clearly an intensional relation between events, that is—a relation between events under descriptions.

It is now possible to reconcile the three theses in the following way: in each case of a psychophysical causation, there exist descriptions of the event-cause and that of the event-effect that can be used to formulate a law; but since these descriptions are physical, the law will also be physical rather than psychophysical. In other words, the reconciliation of the three theses rests upon a claim that the causal relation between mental and physical events, when it exists, is a subordination to a physical rather than a psychophysical law; in this way, the second thesis no longer contradicts the other two. The claim that every mental event that is causally connected to a mental or physical event has a physical description is indeed entailed by this reconciliation. But Davidson goes a step further: he claims that every event is physical. In Davidson's words: every mental event is identical to a physical event.

In order to understand the claim of identity, we must understand the predicates "mental" and "physical". If we define a physical event as one to which a physical predicate can be applied (this, apparently, is Davidson's definition), then the claim proved by Davidson, that every event has a physical description entails the claim that all events are physical. But this definition of a physical event gives rise to a number of difficulties. First, if we take some of our intuitions regarding the concept of a physical event seriously, then we would not say, for example, that the pain I felt yesterday was a physical event; despite the fact that the physical description "occurred after sunrise" is true of it.[16] Furthermore, even if it will someday become clear to us that this feeling is a physical event, it will not be due to the fact that the aforementioned description is true of it. Second, if this is in fact the correct definition, then it is possible to prove the thesis which states that every event is physical without recourse to Davidson's complicated argument, which involves the controversial assumption regarding the anomaly of the mental. This definition leaves the monistic claim so devoid of content that even someone with a dualistic intuition would agree with it. Finally, the main problem with Davidson's definition is that it does not reflect our intuitions regarding physical events or monism. Davidson's argument does prove that every event has a physical description, but since so many descriptions are included in the set of physical descriptions (occurred before a physical event, occurred after a physical event, caused a physical event, the moving of an object, the warming of an object, and others) the conclusion that every event is physical is not warranted.

Such a move would have been more reasonable had Davidson offered a way to pare down the set of descriptions that are considered physical. In other words, if we were to restrict the set of physical descriptions, it would perhaps be justified to adopt a definition in which a physical event is one which can be described physically. Let us take, as an example, an extreme case. Suppose we define a physical description as one which relates solely to a change in an object's location. In such a case, if it were possible to prove that every event has a description as a change in an object's location, the conclusion that every event is physical would certainly seem justified and not merely vacuously true. It would be justified because it is reasonable to claim that a change in an object's location is a physical event.

We can restrict the set of physical descriptions by restricting the set of descriptions in general. Not every combination of words which is true of a particular event constitutes a description of that event. This restriction is necessary in other contexts as well. I will illustrate this in a context which was raised earlier, and will later turn to another example.

As I showed earlier, Davidson refines the claim that causality is subordination under a law, and replaces it by a weaker claim: event *a* is a cause of event *b* if and only if there is a description *P* of *a* and a description *Q* of *b* and a law of nature which states that every time an event *P* takes place, an event *Q* takes place. If every combination of words which is true of *a* can be considered its description, then every two events are causally linked to one another. I will show, for example, that the cause of the outbreak of the Six Day War was the birth of Yitzhak Rabin: Let us describe the event of his birth as an event which occurred before the Six Day War. Let us describe the Six Day War as a war. It is not a random generalization to claim that every time an event takes place that occurred before the Six Day War, a war breaks out. Thus we have subordinated both events to a law, showing that the birth of Yitzhak Rabin caused the Six Day War. Of course, there are numerous ways to reject this example, and even more ways to reject these rejections.[17] I will not discuss this issue at this point. For the purpose of the present argument, this example supports the motivation to restrict the set of expressions that constitute descriptions of events. A restriction that complies with the following constraints is required:

1. An event to which a physical description (in the restricted sense) applies is a physical event.
2. Descriptions which appear in laws belong to the restricted set.

Before presenting my own approach to restricting the set of descriptions, I will show why I do not accept a more obvious approach. On the face of it, we could define a description, in the narrow sense, as one which appears in a law of nature. The flaw in this approach is that it is impossible to define a physical event as one to which a physical description, in the narrow sense, applies. There are two reasons for this.

The first is that our ability to apply the predicate "physical" to an event is independent of our belief in the laws of physics. We know that a certain inflammation is a physical event, even if the expression "inflammation" does not appear (and will never appear) in any law of nature. Further, such a definition of a physical event renders tautological the claim that all physical events are captured by the laws of nature. But there is a logical possibility of there being a physical event which is not captured by these laws. As I claimed in the preceding section, the assumption of the completeness of physics is not a tautology, but an empirical thesis on the possible or prospective development of science.

The second reason for rejecting the proposed definition of a physical event is that it is impossible to expand it in order to define a mental event. This is so since it is clear that not every mental event can be given a mental description which appears in a law. Even if one does not accept Davidson's position that mental expressions do not appear in any law, it cannot be refuted that there are cases in which all the mental descriptions of certain mental events do not appear in a law.

The restriction which I propose is founded on the distinction between sortal and non-sortal predicates. I will review the existing distinction with respect to predicates that apply to objects and expand it to include predicates that apply to events. Every property applying to individuals divides the domain of individuals in two: those to which the property applies and those to which it does not. But there exist several distinctions among properties applying to individuals. One important distinction is that between sortal predicates and other predicates. "Tables", "people", and "pencils" are sortal predicates; "red", "soft", and "made of wood" are not.

I will propose some characterizations of this distinction:

1. We use sortal predicates to count objects. The question "how many tables are in the room?" is perfectly clear, whereas the question "how many red objects are in this room?" is not.

2. When we point to an object, we do so with the help of a sortal predicate. "The table in front of me" refers to an object far more unequivocally than "the red thing in front of me".

3. Attributive predicates are based on sortal predicates. When we attribute an attributive predicate to an object, we must do so relative to a sortal predicate. For example: he is a tall person, but a short basketball player. "Basketball player" and "person" are sortal predicates.

4. A sentence which uses a definite description to refer to a certain object must make use of a sortal predicate. (This characteristic is entailed by the first one, but for my purposes, I am presenting it separately.)

What is analogous to sortal predicates when speaking of events? A sortal predicate indicates a type of object. The same is true of events: murder, collisions, pain and shock are types of events; occurred in the 19th century, occurred in Jerusalem or happened to Joe are not types of events. Let us check whether the characteristics of sortal predicates of objects apply to sortal predicates of events.

1. The question "how many murders took place in 1990?" is perfectly clear, whereas the question "in how many events did Joe participate in 1990?" is not.

2. If it is possible to indicate an event, this is done by using a sortal predicate. "The collision that is in front of us", "this race", but not "that event of Joe's".

3. The dancer danced gracefully, but if during the performance she set off the alarm system in the theatre we cannot deduce that she set off the alarm gracefully. The attributive predicate "gracefully" refers to the sortal predicate "danced".

4. In order for a definite description to refer to an event, it must contain a sortal predicate. "The murder of Julius Caesar" refers to an event; "the event in which Joe participated yesterday" does not.

I propose to restrict descriptions of events to those that attribute sortal predicates to events. Let us call these descriptions sorts of events. We consider the expression "red table" to be a sortal if we accept "table" to be one. Note that in the same way, if the expression "shock" is a sortal predicate, so is the expression "extreme shock". This formulation seems to accord with the intuition expressed by Davidson in the following passage, in which he discusses the problem of the individuation of events:

> I am myself inclined to think we can do as well for events generally as we can do for physical objects generally (which is not very well), and can do much better for sorts of events, like deaths and meetings, just as we can for sorts of physical objects, like tables and people. (Davidson, 1982:137)

Despite the important analogy between events and objects, it is clear that there are differences between them. I presented the distinction between sortal descriptions and descriptions in the broader sense by stretching the analogy between objects and events.[18] We can clarify and sharpen this distinction by a reverse operation: emphasizing the differences between objects and events.

Let us make note of an important difference between events and objects. The sentence "Joe runs" describes (attributes a property to) Joe, but does not attribute a property to the event of Joe's running. Can there be a sentence which describes an event in the same sense in which the sentence "Joe runs" describes Joe? The natural candidate would be a sentence like this one: "Joe's running was fast". The expression "Joe's running" refers to an event, if there exists a single event which is Joe's running. It follows that the sentence "Joe's running was fast" is not an atomic sentence, because its subject is a definite description rather than a proper name. It seems to me to be no coincidence that events, generally, do not have proper names. An event, as opposed to an object, does not change while retaining its identity;[19] it cannot be encountered again, and there is therefore no reason to give it a proper name, just as there is no need to give a name to an object's segment of time. The connection between a sentence and an object is different than that between a sentence and an event. We never indicate an event without using a definite description, and claiming that it has a particular property. When we attribute a property to an event, we refer to the event by using a definite description, rather than a proper name. In light of this analysis, in order to investigate the attribution of properties to events, we will study complex sentences.

According to Davidson's analysis, the most simple claims which attribute properties to events are existential propositions. The logical form of the sentence "Joe runs" is that there is an event which has two properties, the first—pertaining to Joe, and the second—being an act of running.[20] According to the distinction which I proposed, "pertaining to Joe" is a description in the broad sense, whereas "being an act of running" is a sort of event, and therefore a description in the restricted sense. I will illustrate how this distinction is expressed in the logic of events.

Let us consider the sentence: "Joe runs to school quickly". According to Davidson's analysis, this sentence involves an existential quantification over events. It says that there is an event to which four properties apply: pertaining to Joe, being an act of running, being quick and being to school. Do all of these properties have the same logical status? To my mind, "being an act of running" has a different logical function than the other three properties. In order to draw logical inferences from the sentence "Joe runs to school quickly", one need only erase one or more of the properties. For example:

Joe runs quickly.

Joe runs to school.

Someone runs quickly.

Joe runs.

Someone runs.

The word "runs" is preserved in each one of the inferences. If it were possible to erase it as we have done with the other words, we would have to draw the following inferences:

There was an event pertaining to Joe.

There was a quick event.

There was an event to school.

The fact that Davidson's analysis allows such inferences began to arouse criticism as early as 1966, when he first presented his position at a conference on the logic of decision and action. Castaneda's objection to Davidson was that a conclusion of the type "there was an event to school" cannot be formulated in natural language. The preposition "to" gets its meaning from the preceding verb, and thus a claim in which the verb does not appear would be formulated: "There was a to", which is a meaningless claim. Davidson's response to Castaneda (Davidson, 1982:127) was that claims of this sort can be presented as follows: "There was an event involving motion toward".

However, to deduce "there was an event involving motion towards the school" from "Joe runs to school" cannot be justified merely on the grounds of the logical structure of the claims. It therefore seems to me that Davidson's response does not accord with his approach. On the other hand, neither do I agree with Castaneda's claim that these inferences constitute a problem for Davidson. Davidson's response should have been that although the sentence "there was a to" is meaningless, a theory of meaning ought to justify any valid inference in natural language by translating it into a syntactically valid argument in the metalanguage, and not to turn every valid argument in the metalanguage into a valid one in the natural language.[21]

For my purposes, it is interesting to note that it is precisely when we erase a sortal predicate that we arrive at unacceptable inferences in natural language rather than when erasing other kinds of predicates. To my mind, this is because a sortal predicate answers the question "what happened?", whereas other predicates answer different questions, such as "when did *x* happen?" and "how did *x* happen?" In this sense, sortal predicates are more fundamental, and thus sentences which do not have them are frequently unacceptable in natural language.[22]

Let us now check whether the distinction I proposed between descriptions in the broad sense and those which indicate types of events comply with the two aforementioned constraints.

With respect to the first constraint: if an event is of a physical type, then it really is a physical event. If an event is the heating up of an object, that event is physical. If an event is the collision of objects, it is a physical event. But if an event occurred before a physical event or occurred quickly, one clearly cannot deduce that the event was a physical one (in the intuitive sense) despite the fact that these descriptions are also formulated in physical terms.

With respect to the second constraint: a law of nature links the descriptions of events by a proposition such as: "every time an event with the description *A* occurs, an event with the description *B* occurs", or by one such as the following: "every event with the description *A* causes an event with the description *B*", or by weakening the universal claim to a statistical generalization. In all these cases, a law contains the descriptions of events. I am claiming that when one of the descriptions does not indicate a type of event (as was the case in the example of the birth of Yitzhak Rabin and the Six Day War), then the resulting generalization—even if it is not a random one—is not a causal law. I am not offering a definition of a causal law, but pointing out a necessary condition; a causal law must contain expressions which indicate types of events and not descriptions in the broader sense. The intuitive justification of this claim is that the causal effects of an event are dependent on its classification as a type of event, that is, on the question "what happened?" The fact that there is no counterexample to my claim serves as an additional justification. There is no causal law (or candidate for such a law) that links descriptions that do not indicate types of events.

I will now show that Davidson's argument is valid. Let *m* be a mental event which is causally connected to event *e*. According to the third thesis, there is a description of *m* which appears in a causal law. According to the first constraint, this description must contain a sortal predicate, and according to the second thesis, it must be a physical description. Thus a physical description in the restricted sense must apply to *m,* that is, *m* is of a physical type, and following the second constraint, *m* is a physical event.

If this is the case, I propose to strengthen the identity thesis in the following manner: every mental event is a physical event in the sense that it is subordinated under a physical sortal predicate. This sortal predicate, in addition to complying with the logical requirements of sortal predicates, answers the question "what happened in the given event?", as opposed to questions such as when, where or how the event occurred. We can say that a sortal predicate characterizes the event by the type of change that occurred in the participating object or objects.

This stronger version of the identity thesis ensures that every physical event (at least the kind to which a sortal predicate applies) is a physical change in an object. By "a physical change in an object" I mean that an object with the physical property *P* at time t has the property ~*P* at time $t + e$. Only by adding this assumption to Davidson's identity thesis can we use it to prove supervenience$_4$. The proof is as follows:

Let us assume that object *a* has undergone a mental change. That is, at time t_1, object *a* had the mental property *M,* whereas at t_2, it has the mental property ~*M.* This mental change undergone by object *a* is a mental event. We will call it *m.* According to the identity thesis, this event is a physical one, that is, an event to which a physical sortal predicate applies. This predicate characterizes the event as a physical change. We are thus ensured that there was also a physical change. By this I have proved that there is no mental change without a physical one, that is, that supervenience$_4$ is true.

There is no way to apply this argument in order to prove supervenience$_1$, since in the case of two physically indiscernible objects we cannot use the identity thesis to deduce that they are also mentally indiscernible. Let us assume that *a* and *b* are such objects, and that the mental predicate *M* applies to *a* but not to *b*. Even if we can deduce that the event in which *a* is *M* is identical to the physical event *e*, and that the event in which *b* is not *M* is identical to the physical event *f*, we cannot deduce anything from the identity thesis regarding the connection between *e* and *f*. A type-type identity thesis would have allowed us to deduce that *e* and *f* do not belong to the same physical type, therefore deriving a contradiction. But since we are only given a token-token identity thesis, we cannot derive such a contradiction. Thus even the strong identity thesis does not allow us to derive any supervenience other than supervenience$_4$.

To conclude, the three arguments which I have discussed up to this point all share an important characteristic: all three can be seen as a solution to the problem of reconciliation between the following two claims about the relationship between the mental and the physical. According to the first, the physical domain (as opposed to the mental domain) is complete; it is self-sufficient in the sense that it can supply causes and explanations for every event in its domain. According to the second claim, mental events have a true influence on the physical domain. The reconciliation problem arises as a result of the tension between these two claims. Each one of the three arguments interprets them differently, but all three claim that the best way to reconcile the claims is to ensure a strong connection (though not a symmetrical one) between the mental and physical domains.

The connection proposed by Papineau is the supervenience of mental predicates *of events* on the physical predicates *of events*. This is not an interesting supervenience thesis since it does not impose constraints on either mental changes or mental differences between objects. Horgan succeeds in deriving both global supervenience and supervenience$_4$. Therefore he succeeds in imposing constraints on mental changes, but not on mental differences. Davidson derives a token-token identity thesis, the strong version of which can be used to derive supervenience$_4$. Thus, even Davidson ensures constraints only on mental change and not on mental difference. But none of the three arguments have supplied an answer to the following question: can there be two beings with the same physical properties, including the details of their brain's structure, that are completely different as to their mental characteristics?

In the following section I will offer a completely different explanation of the supervenience of the mental. I will not assume anything about the completeness of physics; generally speaking, I will not support my argument on any speculation regarding the possible or future development of physics. The argument I propose will allow me to explain all versions of supervenience, and not only global supervenience and supervenience$_4$, as did (at best) the arguments assuming the completeness of physics.

4.4 An Argument from Justification

As I have shown, the arguments I reviewed above for the supervenience of the mental succeed in grounding, at best, global supervenience and supervenience$_4$; they do not ground the thesis that two physically indiscernible objects are also mentally indiscernible.

Before turning to an attempt to justify this thesis, I will clarify how it should be understood. The difficulty lies in providing an interpretation which will not render the thesis false or vacuously true. By giving different interpretations to the term "physically indiscernible", the thesis can be interpreted in various ways. When claiming that two objects are physically indiscernible, we mean that every physical predicate that is true of the first object is also true of the second. The thesis is thus interpreted differently in accordance with the way in which the set of physical predicates is characterized. On the one hand, if we limit this set to include only intrinsic physical predicates, that is, single-place predicates that attribute a property to an object but fully disregard the object's physical relations with other objects in its environment, then the claim that two physically indiscernible objects are also mentally indiscernible is false. It follows from the arguments put forth by Putnam (1975) and Burge (1979) that if the mental predicates that apply to a particular person are determined by his physical predicates, we must include predicates that describe his or her relations with their environment in the set of physical predicates that apply to the person.

On the other hand, if we impose no restrictions on the set of physical predicates, and allow it to include every open formula in physical language that applies to the person, the thesis becomes uninformative. This is so because two people who are indiscernible with respect to all the physical descriptions that apply to them are one and the same person. I should emphasize that the thesis does not become uninformative by the acceptance of the law of the identity of physical indiscernibles, but by the inclusion, in the set physical predicates, of predicates involving the person's location in space and time and his relations with other objects. However, according to the law of the identity of physical indiscernibles, indiscernibility entails identity even if an object's relations to other objects is not included in the set of predicates. This strong assumption on the identity of indiscernibles is not necessary for rendering the thesis uninformative.

I will now propose an intermediate way of interpreting the supervenience thesis. This interpretation will comply with two constraints: (1) the thesis will not be refuted by Putnam's or Burge's arguments, and (2) the interpretation will not render the thesis vacuously true. The interpretation follows from a restriction of the set of physical predicates to qualitative predicates, that is—predicates which do not refer to space-time or to *specific* objects. Since I am not restricting the set to intrinsic predicates, a *qualitative* description of an object's physical environment will be included in the set of physical predicates. A qualitative description of the environment will include, for example, the predicate: "person x has a blue-eyed father", but not "x's father is y".

In order to clarify my interpretation of the supervenience thesis, I will offer a move similar to Putnam's in the construction of a twin earth (1975:223). There are two differences between my twin earth and Putnam's. The first is that mine will be described solely in physical language. Specifically, Oscar_1's duplicate, Oscar_2, will be indiscernible from Oscar_1 with respect to his physical properties,[23] but I will not determine his mental properties in advance. The other difference is that in my twin earth, the molecular structure of water is H_2O and not *XYZ*. It follows that in my example, Oscar_1 and Oscar_2 are indiscernible with respect to the qualitative physical predicates that are true of them (even those that are not intrinsic), although they are not numerically identical: for example, being located in different places, being born of different mothers.

Since Oscar_1 and Oscar_2 are not identical, that is, they are not the same person, we can ask the following question of them: is every mental predicate that is true of Oscar_1 also true of Oscar_2? According to my interpretation of the supervenience of the mental on the physical, accepting this thesis amounts to answering the question in the affirmative. After clarifying what I mean by the thesis that two physically indiscernible objects are also mentally indiscernible, I will return to the central question of this section: can we justify an acceptance of this thesis? The move I made following Putnam shows that this question is only addressed to those who answer my question about Oscar_2 in the affirmative.[24] A radical dualist would respond that it is possible that Oscar_2's thought and feelings are completely different from those of Oscar_1. I have nothing to say to such a dualist. The challenge I am proposing is only addressed to those claiming that $Oscar_2$ is in the same mental state as $Oscar_1$. The challenge is to explain the source of this intuition and its grounds.

My explanation to this intuition is analogous to the one I offered regarding the supervenience of ethical predicates on natural predicates. This explanation, as well as the argument I will now put forth, are based on an anti-realist assumption. Thus, I am in fact posing a challenge to the realist:[25] it is up to him to propose an alternative explanation of the supervenience of the mental on the physical, one that is at least as satisfactory as my own. In the next chapter I will address the question of whether the realist can meet such a challenge; at the present stage I will limit myself to the construction of the anti-realist argument, one that views the source of supervenience in our procedures of justification. I will begin by presenting an argument whose structure is completely analogous to the one I presented regarding supervenience in ethics (3.3). Some reservations will be addressed subsequently.

The argument's first assumption is that we justify mental claims by using physical ones, or that we justify the attribution of mental predicates to a person by attribution of physical predicates.[26] The second assumption is that truth in the mental domain is identical to justification under ideal conditions; this is the anti-realist assumption regarding the mental domain. The supervenience of the mental on the physical can be derived from these two assumptions in the same way that the supervenience of the ethical on the natural was derived.

Let us assume that the mental predicate *M* is true of $Oscar_1$. It follows from the anti-realist assumption that the attribution of the mental predicate *M* to $Oscar_1$ can be justified. According to the first assumption, this justification will be based solely on the attribution of physical predicates to $Oscar_1$. The same physical predicates are true, we should recall, of $Oscar_2$, therefore justifying the attribution of the mental predicate to $Oscar_2$ as well. It follows from the anti-realist assumption that the mental predicate *M* is indeed true of $Oscar_2$, and thus $Oscar_1$ and $Oscar_2$ are mentally indiscernible.

This argument, like the one in ethics, provides an explanation of supervenience and proves all its versions. The source of the supervenience of mental predicates is in the procedures of justification of claims in this domain, and the source of these procedures lies in the meaning of mental predicates.

But, unlike the argument in the domain of ethics, this argument is open to certain reservations. The main reservation has to do with the first assumption. An observation of the practice of justifying mental claims will reveal that we justify them with the help of behavioral rather than physical claims. Behavioral claims are those whose formulation assumes mental concepts as well. Furthermore, this conclusion does not only follow from an observation of this practice, but also from a look at the meaning of the mental terms and their relations with other terms. The psychological theory that allows us to justify the attribution of mental predicates to others is (predominantly) a theory that explains actions by attributing desires and beliefs. The explained actions are not described neutrally from a psychological point of view, since a pure physical description of these actions does not follow from the attribution of beliefs and desires.

An opponent of this argument would thus argue that I have proved the supervenience of the mental on the behavioral and the physical, but not the supervenience of the mental on the purely physical. *Prima facie,* my argument is nonetheless valid, since all behaviors can be described in pure physical terms (this is the weakest version of the token-token identity thesis). But we must be cautious; it is indeed possible to describe $Oscar_1$'s behavior in physical language, and this physical description applies, therefore, also to $Oscar_2$. But is the move from descriptions of $Oscar_2$ in physical language to descriptions in psychophysical language justified? As long as we do not justify this move, we will be left with an argument which proves the supervenience of mental predicates on the behavioral and physical ones. In fact, the missing link in this argument is the thesis that the behavioral supervenes on the physical. Since the relation of supervenience is transitive,[27] proving this thesis will yield the supervenience of the mental on the physical. In order to prove that the behavioral supervenes on the purely physical, I will describe a systematic ambiguity of behavioral claims. Since these claims contain psychological/mental terms, they are not purely physical claims. The ambiguity I am about to describe pertains to the way in which the behavioral claims contain these terms. I will use the claim "Joe smiled amiably" to present this ambiguity. According to the first interpretation, this claim states that Joe smiled out of a sense of amicability, which was the cause of his smile; according to the second interpretation, however, the claim describes Joe's facial expression without any commitment as to its source.

The difference between the two interpretations becomes evident when we consider our linguistic commitment when claiming that Joe smiled amiably. If it turns out that Joe felt no amicability, we will retreat from the claim's first interpretation, but not from its second one. The first interpretation of the claim requires us to admit that we were mistaken, and that Joe did not smile from a sense of amicability, whereas the second does not entail such an admission: a possible response to the discovery that Joe felt no amicability at the time of his smile is to say that he was just shamming.

It follows that the first interpretation involves mental terms far more strictly than the second. This interpretation logically entails a mental claim. It logically follows from "Joe smiled amiably" that Joe felt amiable at that moment, whereas the second interpretation uses a mental term in order to characterize the way Joe appeared. We characterize Joe's smile as one which looks like the smile of someone who feels amiable without committing ourselves to the fact that Joe is indeed feeling amiable.

There is no need for me to determine which use of behavioral claims is the accepted one. But I am convinced of one thing: in justifying mental claims we can stop at behavioral claims only if we opt for the second interpretation. This is so because by following the chain of justifications and arriving at the claim "Joe smiled amiably" according to the first interpretation, it is legitimate to demand the justification of the belief that Joe felt amicable at the time and therefore the chain will not stop at this point.[28]

If we arrive at the claim "Joe smiled amiably" according to the second interpretation however, the need to justify it is similar to the need to justify the claim "there is a red table in front of me". The chain of justifications stops at "Joe smiled amiably" in the same sense that it does at "here is a red table".

To conclude, I agree with the reservation regarding the way in which I described the justification procedures of mental claims. It is true that one can occasionally stop at claims that are not purely physical, that is, behavioral ones, but only if the second interpretation is adopted.

As I have already mentioned, the second interpretation of "Joe smiled amiably" uses the mental term only in order to describe Joe's appearance, and not to describe the source of his smile, just as the expression "orange" is used in the expression "the scent of an orange" to describe the scent, without any commitment as to its source. There is no reason to think that when we claim that "Joe smiled amiably" we know how to describe Joe's appearance, without using the word amiably,[29] just as there is no reason to think that when we use the expression "the scent of an orange", we know how to describe this scent without using the word "orange".

We know, however, that the claims "Joe smiled amiably" and "there is the scent of an orange" are logically independent of the questions whether Joe felt amiable or whether there is an orange around. In the case of Joe, we know that the claim that he smiled amiably is logically dependent on a specific type of characteristic, such as the angles of the mouth and eyes and so forth. The following claim follows from this knowledge: if Joe smiles amiably then any physical duplicate of his also smiles amiably. Thus the second interpretation of the claim "Joe smiled amiably" obligates us to a claim of the supervenience of the property "smiled amiably" on Joe's purely physical properties. More generally, the second interpretation of behavioral claims necessitates the claim of the supervenience of behavioral predicates on purely physical ones.

We have thus proved the missing link in the argument for the supervenience of the mental on the purely physical. This link will help us complete the argument in the following way:

The first assumption: Mental predicates supervene on the behavioral predicates + the physical predicates. This assumption is based on anti-realism with respect to the mental. My answer to the reservation grounded the claim that the behavioral predicates in this assumption must be interpreted in the second way.

The second assumption: Behavioral predicates (in the second interpretation) supervene on physical predicates.

It thus follows that mental predicates supervene on purely physical ones.

The proof of the supervenience of the mental constructed in this section grounds all versions of supervenience, for the same reason that the analogous proof in ethics grounds all versions of supervenience in that domain (see 3.3). The anti-realist assumption is crucial in this proof; the realist with respect to the mental cannot offer such an explanation for supervenience since he is obligated to preserve the gap between the justification of a claim and its truth.

The proofs for supervenience reviewed in the previous sections are not based on an anti-realist assumption; but they do ground supervenience$_4$ and global supervenience. At this stage, we must conclude that only anti-realism can explain supervenience$_1$, supervenience$_2$ and supervenience$_3$. In the following chapter I will investigate the question whether this situation compels us to accept anti-realism with respect to the mental (assuming supervenience), using the inference to the best explanation.

Notes

1 The claim that these are two different theses is similar to the more familiar claim that an identity thesis regarding events is not the same as one regarding objects. Even when we say that all objects are physical, we have not ensured that all events are physical.

2 Needless to say, this argument is also in dispute, however, it is the subject of a separate, comprehensive discussion.

3 See the general discussion of the connection between supervenience and an identity thesis in section 1.2.

4 I am not arguing that there is no case in which we can derive a supervenience thesis regarding objects from one regarding events. Rather, I am claiming that in order for such a derivation to be valid, additional assumptions must be made about the connection between objects and events, the connection between the properties of events and those of the objects that participate in them, and the connection between the physical properties of an event and the physical properties of an object. As long as Papineau does not supply such a system of connections, such a derivation is unwarranted.

5 Many writers have contested this identification between that which can be imagined and that which is possible: Kripke (1980:104), Stroud (1977:50).

6 Kripke (1980:112, 128, 150)—general discussion on this strategy.

7 I will elaborate on this, using an example, at a later point in this section.

8 Of course, for anyone who does not consider statistical generalizations to be laws (for example Levi, 1964), this possibility does not exist, and a complete theory (in the sense of this definition) must be deterministic.

9 Dretske (1989), Kim (1989), LePore & Loewer (1987), Honderich (1982).

10 The physical predicates that apply to *c* at time *t* include a characterization of the events in *c*'s mind and environment.

11 This is in contrast to Kim's position, for example (1990:1–27).

12 I am here disputing Kripke's claim that we should separate the question of how a particular object could have been from the question of how this object could have changed (Kripke, 1980:114–115). There exists, to my mind, a very close conceptual connection between the two questions.

13 I will later show that it is, in a certain respect, true (section 4.4).

14 To be more specific, this argument proves a somewhat weaker conclusion: that for every two possible worlds which are physically indistinguishable, c is in the same mental state in w_1 as in w_2. But Horgan's argument does not prove that two possible worlds which are physically indistinguishable w_1 and w_2 are mentally indistinguishable in those cases in which the objects in w_1 are not identical to those in w_2. In order to arrive at global supervenience from the conclusion which Horgan proved we must assume that the identity of objects across possible worlds is determined by (supervenes on) their physical properties. (See Lewis 1986:220–248.)

15 This assumption is Davidson's version of the thesis of the completeness of physics.

16 I will later treat the intuition by which "occurred after sunrise" is not a proper description of an event.

17 Davidson raises this problem in "Causal Relations" (1982:158): "It seems unlikely that any simple and natural restrictions on the form of allowable descriptions would meet this difficulty, but since I have abjured the analysis of the causal relation, I shall not pursue the matter here."

18 The distinction is in need of improvement: heating and walking seem to me to be sorts of events, despite the fact that the following questions are problematic: How many times did an object heat up when its temperature rose from zero degrees to a hundred? How many times did I walk when I walked to the grocery store?

19 Strawson (1974) attempts to understand the benefit of giving proper names and the circumstances in which objects have them. He proposes several conditions which must hold. Two of these do not hold for events: 1. The object needs to be identified under different circumstances; 2. The object does not have a definite description that is accessible to anyone who wants to speak of it.

20 Davidson deliberated between two formalizations of such claims. The first of these is: there exists an event which is an act of running and which pertains to Joe (two single-place predicates on events); and the second: there exists an event which is the running of Joe (a relation between an event and an object). I will use the first formalization.

21 I am grateful to Professor Mark Steiner for his help on this complex point.
22 On the importance of sortal predicates of objects rather than events, see Wiggins (1980).
23 Like Putnam, I am restricting myself to qualitative properties. This restriction is necessary for Putnam as well: without it, $Oscar_1$ would be numerically identical to $Oscar_2$.
24 And there are many who do: Haugeland (1982), Lewis (1986), McGinn (1982).
25 Tim Crane (1991b) writes of the tension between the realist approach to the mental and the claim of supervenience, but he focuses on realism in a different sense—the sense in which mental properties exist. Horgan & Timmons (1992) also see the explanation for supervenience as a challenge to the realist, but think that this challenge can be met in the mental domain. The explanation they propose (similar to the one described in 3.3) explains global supervenience and $supervenience_4$, but not $supervenience_1$, $supervenience_2$ or $supervenience_3$.
26 I am dealing, of course, with the attribution of mental predicates to others and not to oneself. Introspection is the subject of a separate discussion.
27 The proof is simple: Let us assume that *A* supervenes on *B* and that *B* supervenes on *C*. If *x* and *y* are indiscernible with respect to the *C*-predicates, then they are also indiscernible with respect to the *B*-predicates and they are thus also indiscernible with respect to the *A*-predicates. Thus *A* also supervenes on *C*.
28 The position by which I can see Joe's amicability without the mediation of any expression or behavior is absurd. I am thus assuming that it is false without, however, arguing against it.
29 To my mind, this fact is the source of the intuitive force of the reservation.

5 From Supervenience to Anti-realism

5.1 The Relationship between Supervenience and Anti-realism

In Chapters Three and Four, I studied various explanations of supervenience. I showed that the only acceptable explanation of supervenience in ethics requires an anti-realist assumption, as does the only explanation covering all the aspects of the supervenience of the mental. In the present chapter, I aim to investigate the possibility of deducing anti-realism from supervenience, using an inference to the best explanation. To this end, I will investigate in what way, if at all, the realist can explain supervenience.

I will begin by discussing Blackburn's argument that the phenomenon of supervenience (at least in ethics), is for the realist, an unsolvable mystery. Referring to various critiques of this argument, I will show that its conclusion is too severe. The following is a more accurate description: supervenience poses a challenge to the realist which, so far, he has not been able to meet. I do not believe, however, that we can determine that the realist cannot, in principle, meet this challenge.

Blackburn's argument (1971, 1984, 1985) derives an anti-realist position with respect to ethical claims from the supervenience of the moral domain on the naturalistic one. In this section, I will present the argument and check whether it is unique to ethics; can the argument be realized, and if so to what extent, in other domains (specifically, in the mental domain)?

Blackburn argues that the moral domain supervenes on the naturalistic one in the following sense: it is necessary that if a particular object is B^* and A, then every object which is B^* is A. (He calls this thesis S.) B^* is the complete characterization of the object from a naturalistic standpoint, and A is an ethical predicate.[1] The above necessity is a conceptual one: it is stronger than physical necessity, and according to Blackburn, it is also stronger than metaphysical necessity. Someone whose moral judgments are not subject to this constraint is not an immoral person; he simply does not understand what a moral value is. It may be possible to explain the source of this constraint, or to derive it from other propositions; Blackburn treats it as a given conceptual "fact".

Blackburn distinguishes between the supervenience of *A* on *B* and the following thesis: every object that is B^* must necessarily be *A* (he calls this thesis *N*). This thesis supplies a naturalist sufficient condition for an ethical property. According to Blackburn, the thesis may be true without expressing a conceptual necessity: it is not a conceptual error to claim that Hitler was a good man; someone who makes this claim is flawed morally, rather than conceptually. The difference between *S* and *N* follows from the fact that it is true of the concept of ethics that if *x* and *y* are identical from a naturalist standpoint, they are also ethically identical. There is no conceptual truth, however, that determines that having certain naturalistic properties is a sufficient condition for morality. Knowing that *N* is true does not only require conceptual capacity, it requires moral capacity.

Blackburn expresses the combination of *S* and the negation of *N* by recourse to conceptually possible worlds. There are possible worlds which contain objects which are B^* and *A*, and others which contain objects which are B^* and not *A*. But there is no possible world which contains objects of both types. Blackburn claims that although this partition of possible worlds is not a contradiction, it is mysterious and requires explanation.

> This is the ban on mixed worlds: it is a ban on inter-world travel by things which are, individually, at home. The problem which I posed is that of finding out the authority behind this ban. (Blackburn, 1985:53–54)

The mystery is created by the fact that a conceptually possible world is one which can be conceived.[2] But if we can conceive a world with an object which is B^* and *A* and one in which an object is B^* and not *A*, why can we not conceive a world which contains both these objects?

Blackburn claims that the projectivist[3] can offer a better explanation of the combination of *S* and the negation of *N* than the realist. Note that if only *S* was considered, it could be given a realistic explanation: the properties *A* and B^* are conceptually related. An object cannot be B^* without being *A*. This connection is part of the meaning of predicate *A*. Clearly, such a connection explains *S* and it is neutral with respect to the realism/anti-realism dispute. The problem is that the explanation does not fit in with the existence of possible worlds which contain objects which are B^* and no *A*. The possibility of such objects refutes the claim of a conceptual connection between the two properties. The only option left to the realist is to claim that the function of ethical propositions is to describe additional aspects of reality. He therefore has no explanation for the fact that these additional aspects are so closely tied to naturalistic aspects.

The anti-realist, by contrast, claims that ethical propositions evaluate a reality that lacks ethical facts; this evaluation will not fulfill its role in our lives if we do not respect the constraint of supervenience. This is, clearly, only the framework of an explanation. Its value depends on the presentation of the roles and on our ability to show that they will not be fulfilled unless the constraint of supervenience is met; for example, if ethical propositions have a behavioral aim, this aim will not be accomplished if, given two physically indiscernible behaviors, one is judged positively and the other negatively.

Blackburn's attempts to offer a more precise content to this type of explanation failed. At no point did he succeed in deriving supervenience from the fact that the aim of moral judgments is not to describe moral reality. The only way to construct a valid argument from projectivism to supervenience is to interpret the projectivist as giving an anti-realist definition of truth in the moral domain, and then to develop the argument that I proposed in section 3.4.[4] If we replace the explanation for supervenience proposed by Blackburn on behalf of the projectivist with the anti-realist explanation offered by me there, we will see that Blackburn's general move does indeed show a clear advantage for the anti-realist. The latter is certainly better able to explain the combination of *S* and the negation of *N* than a realist, who is not entitled to use such an explanation. The main fault of Blackburn's argument lies in the erroneous formulation of the theses and of the mystery of their conjunction. I will offer a more accurate formulation of the theses in order to show that the general thrust of the argument is correct. Under certain conditions, supervenience does indeed constitute a problem for the realist but not for the anti-realist.

We can investigate the formulations with the following question: what kind of property is B^*? According to Blackburn (1984), it is a complete naturalistic characterization of the object. This characterization can be very complex and infinite rather than a systematic predicate; it may well be a predicate that we are unable to capture. In other words, B^* is not one of our concepts. We therefore have no conceptual truths about it. Such truths should follow from the properties of the concept; but if this predicate cannot be conceived by us, what will entail these truths? A related difficulty is that a complex conjunction of naturalistic predicates is not necessarily a naturalistic predicate.

Yet another problem arises from the fact that if B^* is a complete characterization of the object, thesis *S* may become uninformative; this is so since two objects with identical naturalistic characteristics are in fact the same object, and therefore all their other properties are identical, too.[5]

Since Blackburn was aware of this problem, in his later article he proposes to restrict B^* to:

> whatever it is by way of natural or physical states that brings it about that the subject is F... which "underlies" an F state. (Blackburn, 1985:48)

As I showed in endnote 1, this definition is circular, and does not bring us any closer to understanding the concept of supervenience.

If there is no solution to this problem, then S cannot be expressed as a sentence of the first order to which the operator "it is necessary that" is applied. The fact is, we would like to say that for every complete naturalistic characterization B^*, S is true, and in order to do so properties must also be quantified over. Supervenience$_2$ is the version which expresses what Blackburn means by S. I will demonstrate this.

If supervenience$_2$ is true, then for every complete naturalistic characterization B^*, proposition S is true. And conversely: if for every complete naturalistic characterization B^* proposition S is true, supervenience$_2$ is true. This is the case since if x and y are objects indiscernible with respect to the B-predicates, then B^*, the complete characterization of x, is also the characterization of y. Thus if x is A, y is also A. Supervenience$_2$, like S, allows for the existence of "mixed" worlds.

Blackburn claims that the combination of S and the negation of N is a mystery. I proposed that we interpret S as supervenience$_2$. As to the formulation of N, Blackburn oscillates between two interpretations of this thesis. According to the first, with regard to every two possible objects, if both are B then either both are A or neither are A. If all complete characterizations B^* are considered, one obtains a thesis equivalent to supervenience$_3$. The second interpretation yields a stronger thesis, which is committed both to supervenience$_3$ and to the law $(x)\ (B^*x \rightarrow Ax)$. This thesis is stronger since it entails that B^* is given to formulation in our language, and further, that this formulation creates a predicate which appears in laws. According to this interpretation, N is a reductionist thesis.

The two possible interpretations of N create two possible interpretations of the mystery involved in the combination of S and the negation of N. According to the first, the mystery stems from the combination of supervenience$_2$ without supervenience$_3$, whereas according to the second, it results from the combination of supervenience$_2$ (with or without supervenience$_3$) without reduction. Blackburn is clearly inconsistent with regard to this issue and confuses the two combinations with the various challenges to which they give rise. Ultimately, I choose the second interpretation of N, and I will therefore show the "mystery" in the combination of supervenience without reduction. But let us first look at the "mystery" underlying the combination of supervenience$_2$ without supervenience$_3$.

As I showed in Chapter 1, the combination of supervenience$_2$ without supervenience$_3$ is coherent. According to this combination, there are possible worlds in which all the B^* objects are also A, and others in which all the B^* objects are not A; but there are no possible worlds in which some of the B^* objects are A while the others are not.

In light of this analysis, Blackburn raises the following question:

> Why should the possible worlds partition into only the two kinds, and not into the three kinds? It seems on the face of it to offend a principle of plenitude with respect to possibilities, namely that we should allow any which we are not constrained to disallow. (Ibid.:53)

Although Blackburn does not elaborate on this "principle of plenitude" with respect to possibilities, he later offers a different formulation of the question. According to it, the partition of possible worlds into two types rather than three is described thus:

> This is the ban on mixed worlds: it is a ban on inter-world travel by things which are, individually, at home. The problem that which I posed is that of finding out the authority behind this ban. Why the embargo on travel? (Ibid.: 53–54)

Blackburn is mistaken in determining that such an embargo is always a mystery. An object cannot travel to another possible world with all of its properties. I will offer an example of a property with cannot be borne across worlds. Let us define an object as rare iff there are fewer than ten objects to which all of its B-properties apply. The property of rarity supervenes in supervenience$_2$ on the set of B-properties. Clearly, however, there is no law of the type "every object with the property B^* must be rare" (where B^* is a combination of B-predicates). This is precisely the (mysterious) situation described by Blackburn. In every possible world, objects which are duplicates with respect to B are (all of them) either rare or not rare; but an object can be the duplicate of a rare object in our world, while not being rare in its own world. Where does the "embargo" come from? Why can't an object transport its rarity to other possible worlds? This example underscores two facts. The first is that the combination of supervenience$_2$ without supervenience$_3$ is not always mysterious, and the second, that this combination does not contradict realism. Answering the question whether a particular object is rare is no more dependent on our fundamental capacity to know than answering the question whether the object is a triangle.

Even if Blackburn is right in claiming that the combination of supervenience$_2$ without supervenience$_3$ is mysterious, he is mistaken on two fundamental points. First, the "rare" example shows that this combination is not explained by an anti-realist position. Furthermore, as we saw in the previous two chapters, the anti-realist assumption explains the combination of supervenience without reduction, not that of supervenience$_2$ without supervenience$_3$. Second, the combination which holds in ethics is not that of supervenience$_2$ without supervenience$_3$. I agree with Blackburn's critics[6] that all of the reasons for thinking that the ethical supervenes on the natural in follows that the mysteriousness at stake is in the combination of supervenience without reduction. Although this combination is not a formal contradiction, the obvious explanation for supervenience$_2$ and for supervenience$_3$ is blocked by the negation of *N*. The embarrassing question for the realist can be presented as an epistemic one: how do we know that the ethical supervenes on the natural? This is not an empirical proposition; we have not studied pairs of objects such that each time they differed ethically, we discovered that they also differed naturalistically. On the other hand, the negation of *N* refuted the explanation of a conceptual relation between *B*-predicates and *A*-predicates.

It is for this reason that the realist cannot explain the combination: he cannot explain *S* by recourse to *N*. The projectivist, on the other hand, is able to explain *S* in a different way. *A*-predicates are those used to evaluate and judge a reality which contains only *B*-facts. A constraint must be imposed so that such an evaluation does not become a mere whim: the evaluation must provide the same judgments about objects that are identical with respect to *B*.

To conclude, Blackburn's formulation of the mystery in the combination of the *S* and *N* theses was flawed. I have therefore proposed a more accurate formulation of this combination and its theses. The formulation is important because it does not assume that B^* can be expressed in language. The assumption should be avoided because only without it do we have a coherent possibility of supervenience without reduction (see Chapter Two). Should the projectivist position always be preferred to the realist one in all cases in which this combination occurs?

In order to answer this question, I will give a general presentation of Blackburn's argument: the set of *A*-predicates supervene in supervenience$_2$ on the set of *B*-predicates. That is, in every possible world that belongs to *W*, if *x* and *y* are indiscernible with respect to the *B*-predicates, then *x* and *y* are indiscernible with respect to the *A*-predicates. *A*-predicates, however, cannot be defined by recourse to *B*-predicates, that is—there does not exist a combination B^* of *B*-predicates for every *a* predicate in *A* such that *x* is *a* iff *x* is B^* in every possible world that belongs to *W*.

According to Blackburn, the realist is unable to explain this combination. Since the projectivist can explain it, however, we have an argument against realism from supervenience without reduction.

In Chapter Three, I countered Blackburn's claim that projectivism provides an explanation of the "mysterious" combination. I there offered another explanation of supervenience—one which follows from facts about justification with the addition of an anti-realist assumption. If this explanation is satisfactory, Blackburn's argument can be applied to it, and this will yield the following general argument:

If *A* supervenes on *B*, and *A*-propositions are justified by recourse to *B*-propositions, then the anti-realist assumption provides the best possible explanation of supervenience, and we thus have an argument from supervenience to anti-realism.

We can now outline the argument's limits: first, it can only be realized when *A*-propositions are indeed justified by recourse to *B*-propositions. Second, it can only be realized when the realist cannot provide an alternative explanation of the supervenience of *A* on *B*.

In Chapters Three and Four, I showed that there are no satisfactory explanations for supervenience that do not assume anti-realism. Blackburn attempted to go a step further: he tried to show that the realist is in principle unable to provide a satisfactory explanation of supervenience. As we have seen, this move is flawed. But in the following section, I will nonetheless attempt to strengthen Blackburn's claim by studying various schemes of the realistic explanation of supervenience. I will show why these schemes cannot be applied to the domains discussed in the present work.

Before doing so, I will add a clarification. We are apparently faced with two challenges: the first, to provide an explanation of supervenience; the second, to explain the combination of supervenience without reduction. When domain *A* can, in principle, be reduced to domain *B* (in the sense described in Chapter Two), this can provide a realistic explanation of supervenience (or, at least, one that is neutral with respect to realism/anti-realism): domain *A* supervenes on domain *B* since there are conceptual or nomological[7] connections between every *A*-predicate and a combination of *B*-predicates. Such conceptual and nomological connections do not constitute a problem for the realist. Thus supervenience which is accompanied by reduction, or the fundamental possibility of reduction, is not "mysterious" for the realist.[8]

Thus it is only the second challenge, that of explaining supervenience without reduction, that constitutes a problem for the realist.

5.2 An Examination of General Schemes of Realistic Explanations of Supervenience

In the previous section, we saw that Blackburn was unconvincing in his claim that the combination of supervenience without reduction is "mysterious" for the realist: he failed to give a convincing argument for the fact that the realist cannot explain this combination. We shall now examine a number of explanation-schemes that the realist can, in principle, use in order to explain this combination; we will subsequently investigate the extent to which these schemes correspond to the two domains discussed in the present work.

5.2.1 *Forrest*

Forrest (1988) discusses ethics and the predicate "good", yet this discussion can be seen as an example of the more general discussion of supervenience without reduction. His main proposal is that:

> Intrinsic goodness is not, then, a property of the object but of its nature. (Forrest, 1988:2)

In the first stage, Forrest defines the nature of an object. The nature of object x (Nx) is defined thus: the extension of Nx in a possible world w is the set of all the objects in w which are naturalistically indiscernible from x. This is a legitimate way to define a property,[9] and thus x's nature is itself a property of x.

In the next stage of his explanation, Forrest claims that an ethical property is not a property of object x but of its nature—Nx. This claim automatically entails supervenience. In addition, if the ethical property is a contingent property of Nx, that is, a property that applies to Nx in some, but not all, possible worlds; this yields supervenience$_2$ without supervenience$_3$ or reduction.[10] On the other hand, if the ethical property is an essential property, that is, a property that applies to Nx in every possible world, we have supervenience$_3$ without reduction.

In either case, Forrest offers a model for the "mysterious" combination (in Blackburn's eyes) which does not assume anti-realism in ethics. The critical question, to my mind, is whether this model constitutes an explanation of supervenience. The model undoubtedly shows that Blackburn's claim that the very combination is "mysterious" is incorrect, since it shows that the combination is coherent even under a realist assumption. It is possible that Forrest is only interested in showing that the combination is coherent, rather than explaining it; such an interpretation accords with his claim that:

> For while actuality is required to explain actuality, a possibility will explain a possibility. (Ibid.:4)

My object, however, in the present work is to find an explanation of supervenience without reduction rather than merely explaining the possibility of *S* without *R*. In order for an explanation of a possibility to constitute an explanation of an actuality, the assumptions used for the explanation must themselves be reasonable (rather than merely possible). In light of this requirement, we must ask with respect to Forrest's explanation to what extent it is reasonable, rather than merely possible, to assume that "goodness" is a property of *x*'s nature.

Let us now return to the general argument of the present work. I proposed anti-realistic explanations of supervenience without reduction. These explanations were arguments which entailed supervenience as their conclusion. The arguments had assumptions in addition to that of anti-realism.[11] These additional assumptions referred to the justification procedures of supervenience propositions. They are not ad-hoc assumptions: I believe, as do others, (Davidson, 1991:53; Wittgenstein, 1953:580) that they describe the way in which propositions in the given domains are actually justified. Thus the anti-realist explanations I proposed are appropriate to supervenience, and can be referred to by inference to the best possible explanation.

Forrest's explanation, however, is ad-hoc in the following sense: it is not reasonable to assume that "goodness" is a property of the nature of *x*, but not of *x*. One would only entertain such a speculation in the hopes of explaining supervenience. The assumption that "goodness" is a property of the nature of *x* neither explains nor describes other characteristics of ethical discourse. More specifically, it does not explain the epistemology of the field. Forrest claims that the property "goodness" is identified in much the same way as the property "red":

> there is nothing in this account to prevent us being aware of the good-property without being aware of the property to which it belongs. (Ibid.:10)

But this is not a correct description of the way in which an ethical property is identified. We make use of the other properties of an object for such an identification: we refer to the natural properties of an object to justify the attribution of the predicate "good". I find this to be one of the most fundamental facts about ethical knowledge, and it cannot be explained by Forrest's assumption.

To conclude: although Forrest succeeds in showing (via a model) that the very fact of supervenience without reduction is not mysterious, he does not offer a good explanation of this combination. Thus the anti-realist explanation remains the best one.

5.2.2 *Noonan*

In a critique of Blackburn's position, Noonan (1987) claims that there is an additional way to explain this "mystery", without recourse to any anti-realist assumption with respect to the supervening domain. According to Noonan's model, ethical predicates express concepts with a structure which Nozick (1981:51–58) has called "best instantiated realization" (henceforth: B.I.R.). A concept *F* has the structure B.I.R. if there is a series of conditions $C_1, C_2, C_3, C_4, \ldots$ such that each condition in the series constitutes a better way to be *F* than the subsequent one. An object is *F* if it fulfills the best condition to be *F*. That is, an object is F if there is an *i* such that the object is C_i and there is no object which is C_{i-1}.

According to Nozick, the concept of solidity, for example, has the following structure: the conditions in the series describe the density of the object's matter. If there were objects without "holes", then Eddington's table would indeed have been not solid. But since there are no such objects, and since other objects in the world fulfill worse conditions for solidity than the table, the table is solid.

According to Noonan, ethical predicates have the B.I.R. structure when the conditions in the series are formulated in naturalistic language. He claims that ethical predicates therefore supervene on natural ones in supervenience$_2$, rather than supervenience$_3$. Let us examine this.

Let us assume that $N_1, N_2, \ldots$ is a series of natural conditions such that x is M if it fulfills a condition in the series and there is no y that fulfills a previous condition. It is clear that supervenience$_2$ holds, since in every possible world if x and y are indiscernible with respect to their natural properties, and x is M, then y is also M. I believe Noonan is mistaken when he claims that supervenience$_3$ does not hold in his model.

Yet Noonan's claim appears reasonable in light of the following analysis: let us observe x and y in different possible worlds. Object x in w_1 has the same natural properties as y in w_2. They both fulfill exactly the same conditions in the series $N_1, N_2, \ldots$. For example, they both fulfill all the N_i for $i \geq 10$ but not N_i for $i < 10$. Of course, these are not grounds to deduce that if x is M then y is also M: it may be that w_1 may not have an object which is N_7, while w_2 does. This appears to be a situation of supervenience$_2$ without supervenience$_3$. But if we take a further look at the example, we will see that x and y are not indiscernible with respect to the natural predicates, since there is a naturalistic property that applies to x but does not apply to y: $\sim\exists z(N_7 z \& x = x)$.

Noonan (1987:81) responds to this objection by claiming that most philosophers who write about supervenience, and particularly Blackburn, are interested in restricting the set of *B*-predicates, and he therefore allows himself to rule out such properties as $\exists z(N_7 z \& x = x)$. I agree with Noonan that not every formulation in naturalistic language is necessarily a naturalistic predicate that ought to be included in the base set. But a property should not be excluded from the base-set just because it is not intrinsic to the object, but refers to the existence and properties of other objects as well.[12] There is no doubt that in ethics, properties that are external to an action (or to the agent) are relevant to moral judgments. Some examples are the action's results, what the agent thought of the action, the various properties of those influenced by the action, the other options available to the agent, etc. Such properties are very similar to those that Noonan would like to reject, and since these should not be rejected, neither should a property like $\exists z(N_7 z \& x = x)$. If, however, such properties are not rejected, Noonan's model is not an example of supervenience$_2$ without supervenience$_3$. However, as I mentioned in the previous section, it is less important to explain the combination of supervenience$_2$ without supervenience$_3$ (which does not necessarily correspond to our conception of the ethical domain) than to explain supervenience without reduction. The latter is a combination to which Noonan's model is, in fact, suitable.

If Noonan's model expresses everything that is correct about the relation between ethical and naturalistic predicates, then there is no formula θx made up exclusively of naturalistic predicates such that $(x)(\theta x \leftrightarrow Mx)$, and we therefore have a model of supervenience without reduction. Noonan's explanation scheme for this combination is that ethical predicates have the B.I.R. structure. This explanation does not assume anti-realism, since the question which conditions in the series a particular object fulfills and whether there are other objects that fulfill better conditions are questions which may transcend our knowledge capacity.

We must now examine whether the model only describes a possibility, or whether it really explains supervenience in ethics. I agree with Noonan that

> …for any particular concept the claim that it has a best instantiated realization structure will be controversial. (Ibid.:80)

Noonan, like Forrest, is not troubled by the question whether ethical predicates really have the structure B.I.R., since his aim is a critique of Blackburn's stronger theory, according to which the combination of supervenience without reduction is mysterious. But for the purpose of the present work, this question is crucial. It is essential to determine whether Noonan's scheme indeed explains supervenience and not just the possibility of supervenience, and we must therefore check the degree to which the assumptions being used are reasonable. We must therefore ask whether ethical predicates indeed have the B.I.R. structure.

The answer to this question is negative. Among the examples given by Nozick for concepts with this structure (knowledge, justification, personal identity and others) the only convincing example is the concept of solidity.[13] This example is convincing because there is an unequivocal axis of the degree of solidity, and the problem is only determining a point beyond which an object will be solid. Nozick's innovation is in claiming that the solidity of an object is not *exclusively* determined by its place on the axis, but also by the place of other objects. There is no unequivocal axis, however, which can be used to measure the morality of an action. The ethical domain (as opposed to solidity) lacks naturalistic criteria for comparison, that is—criteria that can determine when action *A* is *more ethical* that action *B*. There is no hierarchy of natural conditions ranked by the extent to which these conditions realize the property of morality, and therefore I do not believe that ethical predicates have the B.I.R. structure.

Everything that has been said about ethical predicates is even more true of mental ones. With respect to the discussion of Noonan's position, I conclude that although he has offered an interesting model for explaining supervenience without reduction, the model is not applicable to the domains discussed in the present work; his realistic explanation does not compete with the anti-realistic one that I presented in the previous chapters.

5.3 Implications of the Argument from Supervenience and Its Limits

I have inferred anti-realism from supervenience in both of the domains examined in this work. In this section, I will examine the implications of this inference and its limits. This will mainly involve a comparison of the two domains.

Both domains fulfill three conditions which allow the derivation of anti-realism from supervenience:

1. There is no reduction of *A* to *B* although *A* supervenes on *B*.
2. The anti-realist can explain the above combination.
3. The realist cannot explain this combination.

Anti-realism can be derived from supervenience by an inference to the best possible explanation in any domain in which the above three conditions are fulfilled. For example, it seems to me that the aesthetic domain fulfills all three conditions, and therefore anti-realism can be deduced in that domain. Conversely, even if we accept the thesis of the supervenience of secondary qualities on primary ones, I very much doubt that anti-realism can be derived from this. My argument may fail in the move from supervenience to anti-realism with respect to secondary qualities at two possible stages: first, if secondary qualities are reducible to primary ones (for example, color may be reduced to wavelength), the second condition does not hold. Second, in the case of secondary qualities the anti-realist cannot offer an explanation of supervenience of the kind I proposed in the preceding chapters, since justification procedures with respect to the attribution of secondary qualities vary; we do not always refer to primary qualities in order to justify the attribution of secondary ones, and therefore the second condition does not hold either. This brief discussion demonstrates how to examine whether anti-realism can be deduced with respect to additional domains in which supervenience may hold.

Both domains discussed in the present work allow for an inference from supervenience to anti-realism, which therefore yields an anti-realist concept of truth with respect to these domains. This situation appears similar to Putnam's internal realism.

Putnam's approach is realistic in the following sense: he fully rejects any global relativistic or subjectivist approach. In the ethical and mental domains, a subjectivist approach is particularly flawed: the concept of truth cannot be dismissed in either of these domains. Mental and ethical propositions have truth values, and further, these values are not solely determined by the judging subject. An extreme subjectivist view, by contrast, maintains that even if a proposition has truth value, it is solely determined by the beliefs of the speaker. It is precisely such a position which Putnam rejects. While Putnam distinguishes between thinking that a proposition is true and it being true, the radical subjectivist makes no such distinction. Putnam maintains this distinction by recourse to the singular importance of rationality in the description of the domain; rationality in the sense that a judgment in a domain requires reasons.

I will demonstrate how such a description allows us to maintain the above distinction between a proposition believed to be true and its being true. Let us take for example the judgment that there is no ethical prohibition of single gender marriages. A subjectivist would claim that this judgment is true when the speaker believes that it is true, and false when the speaker believes it to be false. Although Putnam is not committed to the fact that one of these speakers is wrong, his realism is expressed in the fact that we can speak of one of them being mistaken The significance of an error in this ethical judgment is that under epistemically ideal conditions, another position will hold.

There is, clearly, some realist element in maintaining the distinction between the truth of a proposition and the belief that it is true. This element is, however, preserved by Putnam in an anti-realist manner. An error in my judgment does not follow from the difference between reality and my description of it, nor from the fact that a certain state of affairs does not obtain; it is an error in light of the proposition's justification potential. Putnam lends significance to the concept of error via the concept of justification, and therefore truth (the negation of an error) is also defined by recourse to justification. Truth is indeed defined by Putnam as:

> an idealization of rational acceptability. We speak as if there were such things as epistemically ideal conditions, and we call a statement "true" if it would be justified under such conditions. (1981:55)

This is precisely the characterization of anti-realism which I have chosen over the course of this work; it is also the characterization supported by the thesis of supervenience.

There is, however, a significant difference between the way Putnam uses this characterization and the use I make of it. Putnam makes global use of this characterization. According to him, the question of realism is: is truth an epistemic concept in general (rather than in a particular domain)?

According to Putnam, "a truly non-realist view is non-realist all the way down" (1981:57). While I use the epistemic characterization of the question of realism, following Dummet, I see it as a local question.[14] We ask what concept of truth corresponds to a particular domain of propositions.

As I mentioned in Section 2.5, the question whether a global realist or anti-realist position is coherent in any way is controversial. In any event, this work involves a local discussion, and its conclusions are local: a realistic view of truth is not reasonable in either of the domains under discussion.

The anti-realist conclusion shows that the two domains are quite similar. This similarity contradicts the intuition that there is a fundamental difference between them. The intuition is expressed by the fact that it is easier to accept the conclusion that with respect to ethical judgments, the ideal judge is always right, than to accept the parallel conclusion with respect to psychological judgments. This is so because a situation in which x is not in a particular mental state, despite all of the justifications for claiming that he is, is viewed as possible. With respect to the mental domain, it seems to us that independently of the existence or non-existence of justifications, there is a fact of the matter that determines whether someone is in a particular mental state or not.

My conclusion in the present work contradicts the above intuition. In this sense, my conclusion is part of a general trend challenging the existence of an ontological difference between evaluative propositions and descriptive ones.[15] This challenge contributes to our ability to see the strong resemblance between the ethical and the mental domains: both ethical and psychological judgments require justifications; rationality plays an important part in defining the concept of truth in both domains. If we turn back to the more metaphorical discussion of realism (see section 2.5), we see that we are creating, and not merely exposing, truth in both domains. We are interpreting a reality which in itself is poorer, and projecting ethical and mental predicates onto it. We are justified in attributing these predicates, not because we are reflecting reality as it really is, but rather because we are offering a rational interpretation of reality.

The resemblance between the two domains is nicely expressed by Wittgenstein:

> My attitude towards him is an attitude towards a soul. I am not of the opinion that he has a soul. (1953:178)

By attributing the most fundamental predicate to someone: "he has a soul", I am not disclosing anything about him; rather, I am adopting a particular attitude towards him. This attitude contains an element of decision, perhaps even an ethical choice.

I believe this resemblance is both important and fundamental, and is indeed expressed in my argument's conclusion. But whence do we derive the intuition regarding the essential difference between the two domains? I believe the discussion in the previous chapters is instructive here as well. The differences between the two domains are expressed in the differing lines of argument for both, although the conclusion underscores, as I have shown, their similarity.

First, the very intuition regarding supervenience is much stronger in ethics than in the mental domain. I am not merely referring to the "statistical" fact that while certain philosophers deny the supervenience of the mental,[16]

I have not come across any that deny the supervenience of the ethical predicates. Rather, I am claiming that we cannot even *imagine* two people who behave in the same way and argue for the same things, but one of them is moral while the other is not. To imagine a moral person or action is to imagine natural properties that render them moral. On the other hand, we may be able to imagine (at least on the face of it) a situation in which two people are physically indiscernible but one sees red while the other sees green. But this ought not to be taken too far: to imagine this is similar to a situation in which we imagine water that is not H_2O, and such imagination does not ensure possibility. As Kripke shows, when we think we are imagining water that is not H_2O, we are in fact imagining something else (Kripke 1980: 142–143). Thus even supporters of the supervenience of the mental on the physical must argue that to imagine two people in the same physical state who see different colors is, to a certain extent, to entertain an illusion; we imagine a different situation and incorrectly describe the possible world.[17]

This difference in our intuition with respect to the two domains is expressed throughout my argument. For the mental domain, as opposed to the ethical one, there are realistic explanations for some of the versions of supervenience. As I showed in Chapter Four, both Horgan and Davidson can explain supervenience$_4$, and Horgan can also explain global supervenience. These explanations do not assume anti-realism. This difference allows for the possibility of realism with respect to the mental. Since supervenience$_4$ and global supervenience express part of the determinacy we are seeking, they are sufficient for the realist, who can afford to renounce the other versions of supervenience. Such a move is supported by the fact that physical language is so rich and detailed that it is reasonable to assume that some difference can be found between every two separate objects that can be described in physical language. It follows from this that supervenience$_1$ is merely vacuously true. However, as I have shown in section 1.4, it does not follow that supervenience$_3$ is vacuously true, and I am in doubt as to whether this can be said of supervenience$_2$. This is so because even if there are no physical duplicates in our world, their existence is possible, and there is therefore a possible world in which they do exist. With respect to such a world, the question of supervenience$_2$ is not uninformative.

If this is the case, the realist must concede that the mental is in fact determined by the physical, while maintaining that this determinacy is with respect to changes alone. That is, an object cannot change mentally without also changing physically. But the realist must forgo determinacy with respect to differences: he must accept the possibility that physical duplicates may, for example, be able to see different colors. In the ethical domain, conversely, the realist is obliged to give up on any type of determinacy. This is the case since the anti-realist can explain all the versions of supervenience, whereas the realist cannot explain any of them.

The following lies at the root of this difference: the mental plays a causal role in the world whereas the ethical does not. This difference is reflected in the explanations for the supervenience of the mental. Both Davidson and Horgan's explanations make use of this assumption. In Davidson's argument, this assumption is expressed by the thesis that mental events are both the causes and the effects of mental and physical events, whereas in Horgan's argument it is expressed by recourse to the rejection of the epiphenomenalism of the mental. It follows that when domain *A* appears in the causal chain, it is possible, under certain conditions, to explain supervenience without assuming anti-realism, thereby diminishing the power of the inference to the best possible explanation as an argument for anti-realism with respect to that domain. My conclusion fits well with the fact that some of the arguments in the literature for anti-realism in ethics (as well as other domains) is indeed based on the fact that the ethical does not appear in the causal chain.[18] This work expresses the well known fact that the causality of a domain plays a role in our realistic intuition with respect to it in that the only explanations offered for the supervenience of *A* which do not assume anti-realism are those based on *A*'s causal role.

Despite these differences in its details, the argument allows the derivation of anti-realism from supervenience in both of the cases. To conclude, I will attempt to characterize those cases in which such a derivation is possible. My claim is that anti-realism with respect to *A* can be inferred from the supervenience of *A* on *B* under two conditions. The first is that there is no reduction of *A* to *B,* and the second is that *A*-propositions are justified by recourse to *B*-propositions.

The first condition is necessary since if there is a reduction of *A* to *B* then that in itself constitutes an explanation of the supervenience of *A* on *B,* and an anti-realist explanation is rendered extraneous. An example of this is that the fact that the predicate "single" supervenes on the predicate "married" does not justify anti-realism with respect to propositions attributing singleness to people. This is the case since "single" can be defined (or reduced) by recourse to "married".

The second condition is necessary for two reasons. First, when *A*-propositions are not justified by recourse to *B*-propositions, there can be no anti-realist explanation of supervenience. Second, in such cases the realist can propose alternative explanations of the supervenience of *A* on *B:* the supervenience thesis can be an empirical hypothesis. In order to clarify this, let us note an essential point. If *A*-propositions are justified by recourse to *B*-propositions, the supervenience thesis of *A* on *B* is not an empirical thesis, i.e., it is not a thesis that can be learned by experience. This is so because experience cannot refute the thesis: we can never justify our belief that a particular object is A_1 whereas an object which is indiscernible from it with respect to the *B*-predicates is not A_1, since whatever justified our attribution of A_1 to the first object also serves to justify our attribution of A_1 to the second object. In such cases therefore, the thesis of supervenience cannot be explained as an empirical generalization. But if *A*-propositions can be justified independently of *B*-propositions, the realist can attempt to explain the thesis of supervenience as an empirical claim, thus countering the inference to anti-realism as the best possible explanation of supervenience.

Let me once again emphasize that the realist with respect to the mental (or the ethical) can simply deny the thesis of supervenience. In such a case, the argument of this work is entirely irrelevant to him. The realist can refer to the mental or the ethical in the same way that he refers to scientific theory: theoretical propositions are justified by recourse to observational propositions without being reducible to them, but since they do not supervene on the observational propositions, anti-realism cannot be inferred. Theoretical propositions do not supervene on observational ones since there can be a world where the same observational propositions which are true in our world are also true, but the theory explaining them is different from the one which is true in our world. On the face of it, there is no reason to rule out the possibility that phenomena in our world have different causes. Of course, this is a complex issue which I will not delve into at this point, but if I am steering in the right direction, then the present work does not require anti-realism with respect to scientific theories. In any case, it is clear that one of the ways to remain a realist with respect to the ethical and the mental is to reject the thesis of supervenience. The second way is to claim that there is a reduction of the mental to the physical and of the ethical to the natural. The third is to claim that the justification procedures of ethical and mental propositions are different than what I have described.[19]

But if we reject the above three options, and would like to preserve the following three theses:

the mental (ethical) supervenes on the physical (natural);

the mental (ethical) is not reducible to the physical (natural); and

the mental (ethical) is justified by recourse to the physical (natural);

then the conclusion of this work is that we cannot remain realists.

Notes

1 In the 1985 article, Blackburn offers a different definition of B^*: the set of natural properties that underlie property *A*. Since I do not believe the concept of "underlying" can be understood without supervenience, I will not use this characterization. To say that *A* supervenes on *B* is to clarify the intuition that *B*-properties underlie *A*-properties.

2 Conceiving is not exclusively a psychological concept; it is one which is subject to rational constraints.

3 I treat Blackburn's projectivism as a type of anti-realism. Section 3.3 justifies this approach. For the purpose of my main argument, it is not necessary to accept this approach.

4 As was shown in section 3.3.

5 This problem can be resolved, as we saw in section 1.4, by referring to the change of a single object over time, or by referring to supervenience$_3$.

6 Elliot (1987), Klagge (1984), McFetridge (1985).

7 The nature of these connections depends on the nature of the set of possible worlds *W*.

8 In Section 4.2, we raised the possibility that reduction is occasionally not sufficient for an explanation of supervenience.

9 It is significant to Forrest, but not to the present work, that the nature of *x* is not only a property but also a universal, in keeping with Armstrong and Lewis' distinction between properties and universals.

10 The property "rare", introduced in the previous section, is an example of this type of property.

11 Otherwise supervenience would have been entailed by anti-realism—which appears to me incorrect.

12 I discussed reasons for this in Section 1.4.

13 But even here I have reservations: why is the non-existence of a solid object so impossible? And conversely—why might there not be a world in which all objects are solid?

14 Putnam claims (wrongly, I believe) that the anti-realist position offered by Dummett is also global (see Benacerraf & Putnam, 1983:24).

15 Examples: Foot (1958), McDowell (1985), Putnam (1981).

16 Mellor and Crane (1990) for example.

17 Horgan (1987) certainly does this.

18 This is the main argument in Harman's book (1977), for example.

19 McDowell (1985) does this when he claims that ethical and mental truths are in fact perceptual truths, in the sense that ethical and mental judgments need not be justified by reference to other types of propositions.

Bibliography

Ayer, A.J. 1936. *Language Truth and Logic* (Harmonsworth: Pelican Books).

Bacon, J. 1986. 'Supervenience, Necessary Coextension, and Reducibility', *Philosophical Studies* 49:163–176.

Benacerraf, P. & Putnam, H. (eds.) 1983. *Philosophy of Mathematics* (Cambridge: Cambridge University Press).

Bender, J. 1987. 'Supervenience and the Justification of Aesthetic Judgements', *The Journal of Aesthetics and Art Criticism* 46:31–40.

Bennett, J. 1985. 'Adverb-Dropping Inferences and the Lemmon Criterion', in E. Lepore and B. McLaughlin (eds.), *Actions and Events: Perspectives on the Philosophy of Donald Davidson* (Oxford and New York: Basil Blackwell): 193–207.

Blackburn, S. 1971. 'Moral Realism', in J. Casey (ed.), *Morality and Moral Reasoning* (London: Methuen): 101–124.

——. 1984. *Spreading the Word* (Oxford: Clarendon Press).

——. 1985. 'Supervenience Revisited', in I. Hacking (ed.), *Exercises in Analysis* (Cambridge: Cambridge University Press): 45–67.

Brink, D. 1989. *Moral Realism and the Foundations of Ethics* (Cambridge: Cambridge University Press).

Burge, T. 1979. 'Individualism and the Mental', *Midwest Studies in Philosophy* 4:73–121.

——. 1982. 'Other Bodies', in A. Woodfield (ed.), *Thought and Object* (Oxford: Clarendon Press): 97–120.

Carnap, R. 1934. 'The Rejection of Metaphysics', *Psyche: An Annual of General and Linguistic Psychology* 14: 100–111.

Crane, T. 1991a. 'Why Indeed? Papineau on Supervenience', *Analysis* 51:32–37.

——. 1991b. 'All God Has to Do', *Analysis* 51:235–244.

Currie, G. 1990. 'Supervenience, Essentialism and Aesthetic Properties', *Philosophical Studies* 58:243–257.

Dancy, J. 1981. 'On Moral Properties', *Mind* 90:367–385.

Davidson, D. 1982. *Essays on Actions and Events* (Oxford: Clarendon Press).

——. 1991. 'Three Varieties of Knowledge', in A. Griffiths (ed.), *A.J. Ayer Memorial Essays* (Cambridge: Cambridge University Press): 153–166.

Dretske, F. 1989. 'Reasons and Causes', *Philosophical Perspectives* 3:1–15.

Dummett, M. 1978. *Truth and Other Enigmas* (London: Duckworth).

——. 1982. 'Realism', *Synthese* 52:55–112.

Elliot, R. 1987. 'Moral Realism and the Modal Argument', *Analysis* 47:133–137.

Fodor, J. 1974. 'Special Sciences, or the Disunity of Science as a Working Hypothesis', *Synthese* 28:97–115.

Foot, P. 1958. 'Moral Beliefs', *Proceedings of the Aristotelian Society* 59:83–104.

Forrest, P. 1988. 'Supervenience: The Grand-Property Hypotheses', *Australian Journal of Philosophy* 66:1–12.

Goodman, N. 1983. *Fact, Fiction and Forecast,* fourth edition (Indianapolis: Bobbs-Merrill).

Grimes, T.R. 1991. 'Supervenience, Determination and Dependency', *Philosophical Studies* 62:81–92.

Haack, S. 1987. 'Realism', *Synthese* 73:275–300.

Hare, R.M. 1952. *The Language of Morals* (Oxford: Clarendon Press).

——. 1963. *Freedom and Reason* (Oxford: Oxford University Press).

——. 1981. *Moral Thinking* (Oxford: Clarendon Press).

——. 1984. 'Supervenience', *Aristotelian Society* Supp. vol. 58:1–16.

Harman, G. 1977. *The Nature of Morality* (Oxford: Oxford University Press).

Haugeland, J. 1982. 'Weak Supervenience', *American Philosophical Quarterly* 19:93–103.

Hellman, G. & Thompson, F. 1975. 'Physicalism: Ontology, Determination and Reduction', *Journal of Philosophy* 72:551–567.

——. 1977. 'Physicalist Materialism', *Nous* 11:309–345.

Hempel, C.G. 1966. *Philosophy of Natural Science* (New Jersey: Prentice-Hall).

——.1969. 'Reduction: Ontolocial and Linguistic Facets', in S. Morgenbesser, P. Suppes, M. Whit (eds.) *Essays in Honor of Ernest Nagel: Philosophy, Science and Method* (New York: St. Martin's Press) :179–199.

Honderich, T. 1982. 'The Argument for Anomalous Monism', *Analysis* 42:59–64.

Horgan, T. 1981. 'Token Physicalism, Supervenience and the Generality of Physics', *Synthese* 49:395–413.

——. 1983. 'Supervenience and Cosmic Hermeneutics', *Southern Journal of Philosophy* 22:19–38.

——. 1987. 'Supervenient Qualia', *Philosophical Review* 96:491–520.

Horgan, T. and Timmons, M. 1992. 'Troubles on Moral Twin Earth: Moral Queerness Revived', *Synthese* 92:221–260.

Hume, D. 1975 [1777]. *Enquiries Concerning Human Understanding*, (ed.), L.A. Selbybigge (Oxford: Clarendon Press).

James, W. 1970 [1909]. *The Meaning of Truth* (Michigan: Michigan University Press).

Johnston, M. 1985. 'Why Having a Mind Matters', in E. LePore & B. McLaughlin (eds.), *Actions and Events: Perspectives on the Philosophy of Donald Davidson* (Oxford: Basil Blackwell) 1985:408–426.

Kim, J. 1978. 'Supervenience and Nomological Incommensurables', *American Philosophical Quarterly* 15:149–156.

——. 1979. 'Causality, Identity, and Supervenience in the Mind-Body Problem', *Midwest Studies in Philosophy* 4:31–49.

——. 1984. 'Concepts of Supervenience', *Philosophy and Phenomenological Research* 45:153–176.

——. 1989. 'The Myth of Non-Reductive Materialism', *Proceedings and Addresses of the American Philosophical Association* 63:31–47.

——. 1990. 'Supervenience as a Philosophical Concept', *Metaphilosophy* 21:1–27.

Kincaid, H. 1987. 'Supervenience Doesn't Entail Reducibility', *Southern Journal of Philosophy* 25:343–357.

Klagge, J. 1984. 'An Alleged Difficulty Concerning Moral Properties', *Mind* 93: 370–380.

——. 1988. 'Supervenience: Ontological and Ascriptive', *Australasian Journal of Philosophy* 66:461–470.

Kripke, S. 1980. *Naming and Necessity* (Oxford: Basil Blackwell).

LePore, E. & Loewer, B. 1987. 'Mind Matters', *Journal of Philosophy* 84:630–642.

Levi, I. 1969. 'Are Statistical Hypotheses Covering Laws?', *Synthese* 20:296–307.

Lewis, D. 1966. 'An Argument for the Identity Theory', *Journal of Philosophy* 63:17–25.

——. 1986. *On the Plurality of Worlds* (Oxford: Basil Blackwell).

Mackie, J. 1977. *Ethics* (Harmondsworth: Pelican Books).

McDowell, J. 1985. 'Values and Secondary Qualities', in T. Honderich (ed.), *Morality and Objectivity* (London: Routledge and Kegan Paul).

McFetridge, I. 1985. 'Supervenience, Realism, Necessity', *Philosophical Quarterly* 35:245–258.

McGinn, C. 1982. *The Character of Mind* (Oxford: Oxford University Press).

McLaughlin, B. 1985. 'Anomalous Monism and the Irreducibility on the Mental', in E. LePore and B. McLaughlin (eds.), *Actions and Events: Perspectives on the Philosophy of Donald Davidson* (Oxford: Basil Blackwell).

Miller, R. 1991. 'Supervenience is a Two-Way Street', *Journal of Philosophy* 87:695–701.

Moore, G.E. 1922. *Philosophical Studies* (New York: Harcourt, Brace, & Co.).

Nagel, E. 1961. *The Structure of Science* (New York: Hackett).

Noonan, H. 1987. 'Supervenience', *The Philosophical Quarterly* 37:78–85.

Nozick, R. 1981. *Philosophical Explanations* (Cambridge, Massachusetts: Harvard University Press).

Oddie, G. & Tichy, P. 1990. 'Resplicting Properties in the Supervenience Base', *Philosophical Studies* 58:259–269.

Oddie, G. 1991. 'Supervenience, Goodness and Higher Order Universals', *Australasian Journal of Philosophy* 69:20–47.

Papineau, D. 1990. 'Why Supervenience?', *Analysis* 50:66–71.

——. 1991. 'The Reason Why: Response to Crane', *Analysis* 51:37–40.

Peirce, C.S. 1955. *Philosophical Writings of Peirce*, (ed.), J. Buchler (New York: Dover Publications).

Price, A.W. 1986. 'Doubts about Projectivism', *Philosophy* 61:215–226.

Putnam, H. 1975. *Mind, Language, and Reality* (Cambridge: Cambridge University Press).

——. 1978. *Meaning and the Moral Sciences* (Boston: Routledge and Kegan Paul).

——. 1981. *Reason, Truth and History* (Cambridge: Cambridge University Press).

——. 1983. *Realism and Reason* (Cambridge: Cambridge University Press).

Quine, W.V.O. 1953. *From a Logical Point of View* (Cambridge, Massachusetts: Harvard University Press).

——. 1969. *Ontological Relativity and Other Essays* (New York: Columbia University Press):114–138.

Ramsey, F.P. 1990 [1925]. *Philosophical Papers* (ed.), D.H. Mellor (Cambridge: Cambridge University Press).

Ross, D. 1930. *The Right and the Good* (Oxford: Clarendon Press).
Ryle, G. 1949. *The Concept of Mind* (Harmondsworth: Pelican Books).
Sibley, F. 1959. 'Aesthetic Concepts', *Philosophical Review* 68:421–450.
Smart, J.J.C. 1959. 'Sensations and Brain Processes', *Philosophical Review* 68:141–156.
Sober, E. 1982. 'Realism and Independence', *Nous* 16:369–386.
——. 1984. *The Nature of Selection* (Cambridge Mass.: MIT Press).
Strawson, P. 1974. *Subject and Predicate in Logic and Grammar* (London: Methuen).
Stroud, B. 1977. *Hume* (London: Routledge and Kegan Paul).
Teller, P. 1983. 'Comments on Kim's Paper', *Southern Journal of Philosophy* Supp.:51–57.
——. 1985. 'Is Supervenience Just Undisguised Reduction?', *Southern Journal of Philosophy* 23:93–100.
Van Cleve, J. 1990. 'Supervenience and Closure', *Philosophical Studies* 58:225–238.
——. 1992. 'Semantic Supervenience and Referential Indeterminacy', *Journal of Philosophy* 88:344–361.
Van Fraassen, B. 1980. *The Scientific Image* (Oxford: Oxford University Press).
Wiggins, D. 1980. *Sameness and Substance* (Oxford: Basil Blackwell).
Wittgenstein, L. 1953. *Philosophical Investigations* (Oxford: Basil Blackwell).

Index